William Urwick

Nonconformity in Worcester

With an Account of the Congregational Church Meeting in Angel Street Chapel

William Urwick

Nonconformity in Worcester
With an Account of the Congregational Church Meeting in Angel Street Chapel

ISBN/EAN: 9783337209179

Printed in Europe, USA, Canada, Australia, Japan

Cover: Foto ©Lupo / pixelio.de

More available books at **www.hansebooks.com**

NONCONFORMITY IN WORCESTER

THOMAS ROWLEY HILL, J.P.

Mayor of Worcester, 1858.   High Sheriff of Worcestershire, 1870.
M.P. for Worcester, 1874–1884.
Deacon of Angel Street Church from 1858.

Nonconformity in Worcester

WITH

*AN ACCOUNT OF THE CONGREGATIONAL CHURCH
MEETING IN ANGEL STREET CHAPEL,*

AND

*AN APPENDIX OF LISTS OF MINISTERS THROUGHOUT
THE COUNTY, AND EXTRACTS FROM THE
NON-PAROCHIAL REGISTERS.*

BY THE

Rev. WILLIAM URWICK, M.A.

Fellow of the Royal Historical Society, and Author of Nonconformity in Herts,
Bible Truths and Church Errors, a Centenary Memorial *of the
St. Albans Congregational Sunday Schools,
etc. etc.*

London:

SIMPKIN, MARSHALL, HAMILTON, KENT & Co. Ltd.

Worcester:

GREAVES (late OSBORN) Foregate Street.

1897.

PRINTED BY
GEO. W. JONES, 35 ST. BRIDE STREET,
LONDON, E.C.

CONTENTS.

APPENDIX.

PORTRAITS AND ILLUSTRATIONS.

In Memoriam.

IT is with deep sorrow that we here record the departure from this life of our esteemed and beloved friend, at whose suggestion, and by whose request this work has been written,

THOMAS ROWLEY HILL, D.L., J.P.

Of St. Catherine's Hill, Worcester.

We have already (pp. 136-138) given a brief record of the main facts of his life. During the present year his activity was surprising for an octogenarian, and the interest he took in the progress of this work was inspiriting and encouraging. He supplied much material in his own handwriting from the Angel Street Books and other sources. Many letters passed between him and the writer. When in London in June he spent an evening talking over the history and making generous references to friends long since departed; in particular to Mr. RICHARD EVANS and Dr. REDFORD. I visited him in his house, St. Catherine

A

Hill, Worcester, for some days in July, to consult the MSS. in the Cathedral precincts. He had made preparation for my visit, and himself more than once mounted the steep, narrow, winding steps of the EDGAR TOWER to the Muniment Rooms, and introduced me to the Chapter Clerk, Mr. HOOPER, and his assistant. He went to Aberystwith for a week on occasion of the Prince of Wales' and Mr. Gladstone's visit to the Welsh University, and heard, once again, with interest the voice of the veteran statesman, whom he had faithfully followed when in Parliament. In August he visited Folkestone. Alas, he has not lived to see the completion of the work upon which he had set his heart. During September he was struck down by illness, and died on Friday, October 9, 1896, in the faith and love of Jesus. For him we cannot grieve ; he has lived a long and useful life, useful to the end, and he was in harness in Christ's service to the last. He now realizes the promise, *Where I am, there shall also my servant be.* Great is the loss to the Churches, wide the gap his departure leaves among the large circle of kindred and friends who survive him. His remains were committed to the grave in the Worcester Cemetery, on Monday, October 12th, 1896, beside those of his beloved wife, who died four years before him, and amid a large concourse of mourners, representing the Trustees and Deacons of the Angel Street Church, and the public bodies and institutions of the city. His pastor, the Rev. SEPTIMUS MARCH, conducted the service, and gave a brief and touching address, applying to his departed friend the well-known lines of Tennyson, concerning Albert the Good :—

> " Who reverenced his conscience as his king ;
> " Whose glory was, redressing human wrong ;
> " Who spake no slander, no, nor listened to it.
> " . . . . Through all this tract of years,
> " Wearing the white flower of a blameless life ;
> " Laborious for the people and the poor,
> " Beyond all titles, and a household name."

We subjoin a few extracts from the able and valuable obituaries that have appeared in the Worcester newspapers.

HIS WORK IN CONNECTION WITH ANGEL STREET CHURCH.

"THOMAS ROWLEY HILL began in very early life his connection with religious work as a Sunday School teacher, and also as the teacher of a Bible Class held in the old Athenæum, which stood near Foregate Street, a little below the present railway bridge. It was in 1834 that he became a member of Angel Street Church, and since then he has been one of its most active and devoted supporters. His sound judgment, his sincere religious earnestness, the union in him of wise firmness with an amiable and kindly temper, all combined to make him invaluable in the conduct of the business of the Church, especially when from time to time it has had to regret the removal of higly esteemed ministers. Mr. Hill was for a great number of years a member of the diaconate, being for a large part of the time senior deacon, and took a very active interest in the work of the Church. He often read the lessons, and those who have listened to him on those occasions were greatly

impressed with the clear tones and reverential spirit in which
he performed that duty.   "He was one of the best readers of
Scripture I have ever heard" is the comment of one who knew
him well as a helper in the services.   The financial aid which
he gave in the re-building of the chapel, the schools, the class-
room, the church parlour, and the Manse at Battenhall, together
with his regular contributions to the local work of the Church
and its branches, would amount to a princely sum, to say
nothing of the handsome donations which he gave to the Congregational Churches in Malvern, Broadway, and in most other
towns in the county.   His help was valued not only because of
its intrinsic worth, but because of the encouraging stimulus it
gave to others to in some degree follow his noble example.
He gave largely to the London Missionary Society, the Church
Aid Fund, and the Home and Colonial Mission Fund—indeed
it is but a few weeks since we recorded his gift of £1,000 to
the first named society."—*Borrow's Worcester Journal*, Oct. 10,
1896.

Help to Episcopalians.

"But while he was generous to Nonconformist objects, his
purse was often at disposal for other denominations.   He gave
help to the restoration of the Cathedral, the Cathedral School,
and St. Helen's Church, and was a very generous donor
(£1,300) to the fund for the re-building of Suckley Church in
1879.   Up to 1883 the living of St. Andrew's, in this city, was
about £75 a year, towards altering which, good Churchmen
in the parish had repeatedly tried and failed.   The matter was
brought to the notice of Mr. Rowley Hill, who exerted himself
energetically to bring influence to bear upon the Ecclesiastical
Commissioners, and an accumulated fund of some £3,700

(which had been left by a wealthy Worcester lady for the purpose of supplementing the incomes of poor clergymen in the city) was brought to light, and assigned to St. Andrew's parish, thereby raising the stipend of the Rector to something like £240 a year.—*Borrow's Worcester Journal*, Oct. 10, 1896.

His Efforts in Promotion of Education.

The British Schools, Worcester, were established at the beginning of the century and have been supported by friends of education belonging to all the Christian Denominations For fifty-six years Mr. T. Rowley Hill contributed liberally to the Funds as an Annual Subscriber ; and as an Active Manager and President of the Schools for many years, he always took a practical and deep interest in their welfare, encouraging all connected with them with his own kindly influence. In illustration of this it may be mentioned that Mr. Hill has been accustomed at the Annual Prize Distribution, to present every child who had made full attendances during the year, with a new half-crown; and the number increased each year accordingly.

In the year 1892, consequent upon the requirements of the Education Department, it was found necessary to make great structural alterations in the school buildings. Mr. Hill threw himself heartily into this work, and by his own example emphasized his influence upon others. He purchased at a heavy cost, and then presented the site for a new Girls' and Infants' School premises ; out of a total cost of £3952 he contributed £2300 ; and thus the work of renovating the Boys' School, and providing new schools for the Girls and Infants, with an increased accommodation for 270 children, is entirely paid for. The managers in recognition of the munificent kindness of Mr.

Hill, erected a Brass Mural Tablet in the Boys' Schoolroom, bearing the following inscription :—

British Schools.

This Tablet, erected by the Managers
of these Schools, gratefully records
their indebtedness to the munificence of
Alderman T. Rowley Hill, D.L., J.P.,
the originator of and principal contributor to
the Renovation of the Boys' Schools, and the erection
of the New Premises for Girls and Infants.

May 31st, 1894.

This was formally unveiled by Miss Westcombe on the occasion of the opening ceremonies on that date when GEO. H. WILLIAMSON, Esq. Mayor of Worcester, presided. Mr. T. Rowley Hill was present, and " feelingly acknowledged the kindness which had been shown towards him, and the honour conferred upon him by the erection of the tablet. He also gratefully acknowledged the assistance which had been given by all their friends in carrying out that work. They had all worked together harmoniously and energetically, and those who had been specially charged with official duties, the Treasurer, Mr. E. P. EVANS, and the Secretary, Mr. GEO. LEWIS, had devoted a great deal of time and care to the work. They were also much indebted to Mr. BERRY, the Head Master, and the Ladies' Committee, for the energetic support they had given to the enterprise." Thus he evinced the charming grace of his character, as he took the honour due to himself to place it at once on the shoulders of others.

At a Meeting of the Committee of Managers on Tuesday, Oct. 27th, 1896, Mr. GEORGE LEWIS presiding, the following resolution was passed unanimously : " That we sorrowfully .

record the death of our venerable, respected, and beloved president, Mr. T. Rowley Hill, whose munificent generosity this splendid block of school buildings attests, whose kindly sympathy with the work carried on here his manifold deeds of goodness prove, but whose many excellences it were impossible to enumerate. For 56 years Mr. T. Rowley Hill was a liberal subscriber to the funds of this school, for over 35 years an active member of this Committee of Management, and for over 20 years the honoured President. As a committee we gladly recall the pleasure we have derived from our intercourse with him here through so many years—the value of his counsel, the accuracy of his judgment, the largeness of his heart, with the teachers his sympathy, with the children his kindliness, and with all his benevolent influence. And as we cherish his memory and seek to carry on the work here, in whose welfare he loved to take such deep interest, we acknowledge that the loss we have sustained by his removal we cannot adequately express. Resolved further, that we desire to express our condolence with the family of the late Mr. T. Rowley Hill in sending them a copy of the foregoing resolution."—*Furnished by Mr. E. Berry, the Head Master.*

He was CHAIRMAN of the WORCESTER SCHOOL BOARD, and a member of the Suckley District School Board, and chairman of the Governing Body of the Boys' and Girls' BRITISH SCHOOLS at St. Martin's Gate. In the original building of these schools he had a part, and for the building of the girls' school in connection therewith, in 1893, he gave the site, valued at £700, and towards the building fund £1000. He was one of the most prominent promoters of the LIBRARY movement in Worcester, and later of the VICTORIA INSTITUTE scheme, the successful completion of which owes much to his generosity and influence. He was once secretary to the Old City Library, which formed the nucleus of the Public Library, and subscribed £500 towards the cost of establishing the Free Public Library on the adoption of the Public Libraries Act. He was one of the first subscribers, of £1000, to the Victoria Institute scheme, and since contributed an additional £500, the last subscription being in response to a special appeal in 1894, when the foundation stone of the Institute was laid. It was a recognition to his devotion to the promotion of education that he was elected in November, 1887, one of the Six masters, the governing body of the Royal Free Grammar School, and it is worth noticing that he was the first Nonconformist elected on that body. By this his interest in education, shown by his part in the maintenance of the British Schools and the School Board of which he was chairman up to 1886, was extended to the old endowed schools of the city, with the interests of which he further identified himself by a noble subscription of £1000 towards augmenting the endowment of the Cathedral School.

Mr. Hill's disinterested and splendid services to the city in a variety of capacities was recognised by a public testimonial in 1881. The testimonial took the form of a portrait, and there were 989 subscribers. The portrait, which represents Mr. Hill in the House of Commons, was painted by Mr. Frank Holl, and was hung in the Guildhall at a large public gathering on Sept. 27, 1881. It bears this inscription : "This portrait of Alderman Thomas Rowley Hill, M.P., was painted by means of subscriptions given by his friends and fellow citizens, and was placed in the Assembly Room, Guildhall, in recognition of his private worth and distinguished public services to the citizens of Worcester during his long life among them, of the thorough identification of himself with the interests of the city and county of Worcester, and of the affectionate esteem felt for him by all classes.—Sept. 27, 1881."—*Ibid.*

IN BEHALF OF GENERAL CITY CHARITIES.

In the Royal Albert ORPHAN ASYLUM at Henwick, Mr. Hill always took a special interest. He was one of the three trustees, and a prominent member of the committee, at whose periodical meetings, he also invariably acted as chairman. He was an annual subscriber, whilst his munificent donations to the institution can best be measured by the fact that he was by them entitled to no less than 67 life votes. He had given no less than £1325 to the Asylum, while the late Mrs. Hill had also given £200. But what to many will count as more than financial aid the most bountiful, was the ever ready sympathy and cheerful kindliness which he displayed in all affairs of the Asylum, in which and its youthful inmates he always took so fatherly an interest. He was a frequent and ever welcome visitor.

Mr. Hill was a Vice-President of the Worcester GENERAL INFIRMARY, amongst whose life-governors he was numbered by reason of his donation of £100 to its funds, and he was at one time a member of the Executive Committee. He showed his approval of the efforts made recently to raise a special fund for providing a NURSES HOME in connection with that institution by a generous donation of £50.

Very little known to the public is one good instance of Mr. Hill's munificence. Twenty years ago or more he established some ALMSHOUSES in the Bath Road. The houses, of which there were four, are of a good size, and were built especially for the purpose. They are for aged women, and each of the occupants receives seven or eight shillings a week.

He contributed £100 towards the erection of the new RAIL-WAY MISSION HALL in East Street, which was recently opened; and in the foundation stone-laying proceedings of which he took part. It were impossible even to mention all the public charities and charitable societies to which Mr. Hill was a regular subscriber. In fact he helped practically everything of a useful character in the city.—*Worcester Chronicle*, Oct. 10, 1896.

"The PUBLIC LIBRARY movement might not for many years to come have been brought to a successful issue, but for the impetus it received from Mr. Hill, and his offer of a site near the Public Hall; and although that site was not adopted, the ready support he gave to the suggestion that the value of the site should be a cash contribution to the securing of another site, rendered great help in making it possible to carry on the movement. From time to time, at critical points, when it seemed likely that the whole movement would collapse, Mr. Hill came forward with renewed and liberal efforts; which not only added substantially to the funds of the committee, but incited other liberal-minded men to give contributions also. Mr. Hill during his lifetime declined, with his natural shrinking self-effacement, to have his name connected with any part of the building, but his death has removed all such barriers to the recognition of his services, and they were able now to fully give vent to their inclinations in doing honour to one who had done so much service for the city. The dramatic coincidence of his death, with the opening of the institute would inseparably connect his name with the Victoria Institute. Whatever the City Council or they themselves decided upon, it was true that the memorial of a long and glorious reign would also be the monument of one who had during the greater portion of that reign been one of the most eminent and useful citizens of Worcester."—*Speech of* Mr. FREDERICK CORBET ; *Worcestershire Chronicle*, Oct. 24, 1896.

Reference was made to his death, in Worcester Cathedral by Canon KNOX-LITTLE ; at the Countess of Huntingdon's Church, by the Rev. E. J. BOON ; in the Sansome Walk Chapel, by the Rev. FORBES JACKSON, of Reading ; in St. Michael's Church, by the Revs. M. T. SPENCER and R. THURSFIELD ; by the vicar of St. Paul's, the Hon. H. DOUGLAS ; by the Rev. A. MAITLAND in St. Martin's. Funeral sermons were preached in Angel Street Chapel, by the Rev. SEPTIMUS MARCH ; in Park Street Chapel, by the Rev. F. J. YEATS ; in St. Clement's, by the Rev. F. H. RICHINGS. Resolutions of respect and appreciation were adopted by the Worcester Liberal Association, the Infirmary Committee, the County Justices, Knightwick Farmers' Association, Public Library Committee, Cathedral School Governors, Association of Worcester Free Churches.

FUNERAL SERMON BY THE REV. SEPTIMUS MARCH, in Angel Street Chapel, Oct. 18, 1896.

The preacher gave out as his text Job v. 26, "Thou shalt come to thy grave in a full age, like as a shock of corn cometh in in its season." That had been so in the case of their departed friend, who had gone to his grave in his full age. It was not of the circumstances, historical or biographical, or of the details of his life, said Mr. March, that he would speak that morning, but rather of his character—not the environment, but the man. The late Mr. Hill had been what was usually called successful, and he wished to speak (i) of the characteristics that led to that success, and then (ii) the characteristics which accompanied it. Their friend had been characterised by *diligence*—the speaker had never known him idle ; and he was also marked by *punctuality*, and was always *methodical* and *prompt.* His correspondence he had attended to the first thing in the morning with rapidity and terseness. Another characteristic was *thrift.* He knew how to husband his resources and disliked wastefulness and extravagance. *Decision* of character had also marked the late Mr. Hill. He did not spend his time weighing the *pros and cons* of a subject, but almost by intuition arrived at his conclusions, and would give a decided "Yes" or "No." He had, moreover, *a strong will.* Those who had strong wills were in danger of obstinacy, which had been rightly defined as "Will asserting itself, but unable to justify itself." But if Mr. Hill ever found he could not justify his attitude on any subject he would come round and repent, perhaps not in words, but in actions. He was also characterised by strict *integrity*, always upholding the motto that "Honesty is the best policy."

Many people had these characteristics, and by them had climbed to large success. But they had not possessed the further characteristics (ii) which had accompanied their friend's success. If they had possessed them, when they became successful they had gradually lost them, because many were the perils and spiritual dangers which beset a prosperous man. In his success Mr. Hill had been characterised by *generosity.* Their friend had given out of his abundance ; yet no one was more ready than he to do honour to those who "gave the widow's mite," and gave out of their penury. Nevertheless, he was certainly a most generous man. It was in truth, a somewhat rare characteristic, for the more men got, the more loth were they to part with what they had. The personal ambitions grew ; so when one saw a noble exception, it was well to mark it. Mr. Hill's generosity had been *thoughtful*, not impulsive. He thought matters over, and gave

with *discrimination*, and *unostentatiously*. When he gave not
anonymously he wanted to stimulate the generosity of others,
but there were many quiet, unseen rills of liberality which had
trickled here and there, bringing comfort and cheer to the poor
and sad. Another characteristic was *humility* before God.
The *De Profundis* (Psalm 130) which they had heard that morning was one of the two Psalms which Mr. Hill had asked
should be read to him on his bed of suffering. *Love and affection*, too, had characterised their late friend, who, if he had not
worn his heart upon his sleeve, possessed one nevertheless.
If the well was deep the water when reached was sweet. He
had *faith in man*—that was to say, if he trusted a man he
trusted him out and out. And with faith in man went *loyalty*
—loyalty to his country, to his Sovereign, the Christian Church
here, and the preacher might add, to him also as his minister.

Mr. Hill had something better—*faith in God*. Early in life he
gave his heart to Christ, resolved to do His bidding come what
might. Every day he looked into God's Word, spoke with
Him, took counsel with Him. And so he lived uprightly, the
seed thus early planted in good soil having struck root, had
grown, developed, and ripened. For eleven years Mr. Hill had
represented the city in Parliament, and how well he did it ! and
at the end of those eleven years he was rejected. But he did not
thereupon say he would have "nothing more to do with these
people," nor had he manifested any resentment ; he set himself
to do all he could for the advantage of his fellow citizens, and
so the city had been perhaps the gainer by that rejection.
Eleven years of life remained to him, and during those years he
cared for the culture of his own soul at the same time that he
cared for the interests of those round about him. Six years
ago Mr. Hill lost his wife, the partner of so many changeful
years, and the mother of his children. Then his sons and

daughters,* having passed from under the parental roof one by
one, and his wife gone, a certain lonesomeness fell upon
him. Yet

> " He was not all unhappy, his resolve
> Upbore him, and firm faith and evermore
> Prayer from a living source within the veil
> Kept him a living soul."

The preacher passed on to Mr. Hill's last illness, when after a
while his mind seemed clouded and lost to impressions of the
outer world. On the afternoon of the day of his death, the
preacher said he had gone into the silent room and had gazed
upon the face which bore a look of exceeding gentleness. The
old lines of strength, and force, and rugged vigour seemed
smoothed out. "Now abideth these three, faith, hope, and
love—the greatest of these is love "—he had reached his per-
fection. Such, added Mr. March, was his word-picture of
Thomas Rowley Hill. Some it would not satisfy, they would
think he had put too much or too little colour into it, and that
light and shade were not properly balanced—he could not help
it. It was as he had known him those nineteen years. He
hoped that they might all derive some lessons of usefulness as
they gazed upon the past. And their friend was now gone into
his grave, or rather through the grave to his Eternal Home, in
a full age, like as a shock of corn cometh in in his season."

The Pastor delivered the closing words with evident emotion,
which was shared by all as the words of the grand hymn,
" Lead, Kindly Light," rose and filled the chapel.

The Blessing was then given, and all stood in solemn silence
as Mr. L. G. Winter, who had presided at the organ, played

* Mr. Hill leaves two sons and two daughters.—Mr. THOMAS W. HILL, of Froxmere
Court, Crowle, Mr. E. HENRY HILL, of Broadwas Court, Mrs. KANE, wife of the Rev.
R. N. KANE, Rector of Suckley, and Mrs. WILSON, wife of the Rev. J. WILSON, Rector
of Knightwick.

the Dead March in "Saul," with which the service ended.—
The Worcestershire Congregational Magazine, October, 1896.

MEMORIAL SERVICE AT MALVERN.

There was an overflowing congregation at Holly Mount Congregational Church, Malvern, on Sunday morning, Oct. 18, when
a service was held in memory of the late Mr. Thomas Rowley
Hill. Appropriate hymns were sung, and the sermon was
preached by the pastor, Rev. WALTER LEE (Secretary of the
Worcestershire Congregational Union), who took for his text
Hebrews xi., 4, "He being dead yet speaketh." After referring to the patient way in which Mr. Rowley Hill had borne his
last illness, the preacher said : During that time and while
his faculties were still clear, he frequently requested the Bible
to be read to him, and would himself point out the family
portions. He also liked to hear some of his favorite hymns.
The last passage of Scripture which he was heard to utter
(this with much feeling) was the beautiful and significant verse,
"The darkness is past and the true light now shineth." Yes ;
whatever of doubt or difficulty, or darkness, there had been in
his life, all these had disappeared in the chamber of his affliction. The true light now shineth—the light of faith and hope
and love revealed to him, in the presence of that Saviour whom
he had loved and faithfully served for more than 60 years.
The city and county of Worcester mourn the loss of a true
gentleman, a simple, earnest, diligent, upright statesman, a
municipal philanthropist, a humble, faithful, noble Christian ;
and we in the Church, who knew him well and remember his
many kindnesses to our Church, and his profound interest in
our welfare, likewise mourn his loss, and join in expressions of
respectful sympathy and condolence with the members of the

bereaved family. "He being dead yet speaketh." His character, his example, his influence, yet speak for him and of him, and speak to each of us, saying, "Go thou and do likewise."

Among the characteristics of his life were his remarkable sense of stewardship with regard to the possession and use of his wealth, his time, his talents, and his energy, and his fidelity to convictions, especially with regard to his political and ecclesiastical principles. None could fail to observe his unaffected modesty and humility; there was not a trace of vanity or pride within him. Finally, there was his devoutness of life. He was a man of prayer; he conducted family worship in his house morning and evening regularly. They thanked God for the noble and useful life which Mr. Rowley Hill was enabled to live—for the ripe old age to which he was spared—for the preservation of his faculties to within a few days of his end, and, above all, for the inspiring example he has left to speak for him to his family, and to all men.—*Worcestershire Chronicle,* Oct. 24, 1896.

NONCONFORMITY IN WORCESTER

*With an Account of the Congregational Church,
and Lists Referring to the County.*

I.

A Worcestershire Lollard Martyr.

THE Protestant Nonconformists of England trace
their origin to and take their stand upon THE
HOLY SCRIPTURES as containing all things
necessary to salvation, teaching renewal of
the Holy Spirit, and redemption through our
Lord Jesus Christ, in opposition to the Ecclesiastical figment
of apostolical succession, and miracle-working priests who, in
the sacraments of baptism and the eucharist, give by magic
regeneration and spiritual life. Nonconformists go back to
the Reformers before the Reformation, and find their spiritual

B

forerunners in Wyclif and the Lollards. Worcestershire can boast of its Lollard martyr, JOHN BADBY by name. In an old chapel of Worcester Cathedral called the *Carnaria,* dedicated to Thomas à Becket,* and probably in the crypt, on Saturday, the 2nd of January, 1409, sat the reverend father in God, Thomas Peverell, lord bishop of Worcester, holding his court as chief judge ; and before him the accused, a Lollard named JOHN BADBY, a Worcestershire man of good family (for Robert Badby had held the honourable office of Escheator for the county in 1389-90†), described as *faber,* which Foxe renders *Artificer,* "a layman of Evesham in the county of Worcester." He is accused of maintaining what Nonconformists still maintain in the face of sacerdotalism :—

> That the sacrament of the body of Christ consecrated by the priest upon the altar is NOT the true body of Christ by virtue of the words of the sacrament, but that after the sacramental words spoken by the priest, the material bread doth remain upon the altar as in the beginning. John Badby said expressly, he would never while he lived believe that any priest could make the body of Christ sacramentally ; that when Christ sat at supper with his disciples He had not his body in his hand.

Bishop Peverell having by threats and persuasions endeavoured in vain to move the culprit, gave sentence, pronounced Badby a heretic, and sent him to headquarters. When

---

* Valentine Green's *History of Worcester,* I., 98.
† Nash's *Worcestershire,* Int. 13.

THE BURNING OF THE LOLLARD, JOHN BADBY.
A Worcestershire Man. A.D. 1409.

brought before the Archbishop of Canterbury in London, Badby said, " he would believe in the omnipotent God in Trinity; but if every *host* being consecrated at the altar were the Lord's body, there would be twenty thousand gods in England." The Archbishop in St. Paul's ratified the Bishop of Worcester's sentence, and handed the heretic to the secular power.

In the afternoon of Wednesday, March 5, 1409, John Badby, the Worcestershire artificer and layman was brought to Smithfield, and there, being put into an empty barrel, was bound with iron chains fastened to a stake, having dry wood put about him. Meantime, the prior of St. Bartholomew's in Smithfield, brought the *host*, in great pomp, with twelve torches borne before, and held it up to their poor victim at the stake, demanding how he believed in it. " I know well," he replied, " it is hallowed bread, but not God's body." And then was the tun put over him and the fire kindled. When the innocent soul felt the fire he cried " Mercy ! " calling upon the Lord ; and the prince, the king's eldest son, looking on, ordered them to quench the fire, and offered him life and a yearly stipend if he would forsake heresy and accept the faith of holy church. But, continues Foxe, " this valiant champion for Christ, neglecting the prince's fair words, being fully determined rather to suffer any kind of torment than so great idolatry and wickedness, refused the offer of worldly promises. He persevered invincibly to the end, not without a great and most cruel battle, but with much greater triumph of victory ; the Spirit of Christ having always the upper hand in His members, maugre the fury, rage and power of the whole world." *

Nearly five centuries have passed since JOHN BADBY, layman of Evesham, in Worcestershire, was tried and condemned in Thomas à Becket chapel in Worcester Cathedral. But while the error which he rejected is still maintained by many ecclesiastics of the English Establishment, thank God, the truth and firmness of the martyr, and the simplicity of the Gospel he confessed, are the watchwords of English Nonconformity in Worcester and in Britain still. As Wyclif exclaimed, THE TRUTH MUST PREVAIL.

* Foxe, *Acts and Monuments,* Townsend Ed. III., 239. Wilkins' *Concilia,* iii., p. 234.

II.

The Martyr Bishops of Worcester.

WORCESTER as a cathedral city possesses the honourable distinction of having among its bishops the two most noble Protestant martyr-bishops of the English Reformation, HUGH LATIMER and JOHN HOOPER.

HUGH LATIMER was born about the year 1491 at Thurcaston, in the county of Leicester, where his father was a yeoman farmer. At the age of 14 years he went to Cambridge, took B.A., and a fellowship of Clare Hall, in 1510. He took orders at Lincoln, was zealous in the Popish religion, and preached against Philip Melancthon in 1524.[*] About this time he formed a friendship which led to his

---

[*] Foxe, *Acts and Monuments*, Townsend's Ed., VII., 437; *Memoir* by G. E. Corrie, Parker Soc.; Cooper, *Athenæ Cantab.*, I., 30.

conversion.   He used to walk in the fields with the martyr
Thomas Bilney, of Trinity Hall.   Latimer writes:—

> "Master Bilney, or rather Saint Bilney, that suffered death
> for God sake, was the instrument whereby God called me to
> knowledge. For I may thank him, next to God, for that
> knowledge that I have in the Word of God. For I was as
> obstinate a papist as any was in England. Bilney came to my
> study at Cambridge, and desired me for God's sake to hear his
> confession. I did so, and to say the truth, by his confession I
> learned more than afore in many years. So from that time
> forward I began to smell the Word of God and forsake the
> school doctors and such fooleries." *

In December 1530 Latimer addressed a very able and
eloquent letter to Henry VIII., urging FREE LIBERTY OF
READING THE HOLY SCRIPTURES.   In August 1535 he was
elected bishop of Worcester, and consecrated during the
ensuing month.†   "Here," says Foxe,‡ "he continued,
instructing his diocese according to the duty of a diligent
and vigilant pastor," giving the following lines to say to
communicants at the communion :—

> Of Christ's body this is a TOKEN,
> Which on the cross for your sins was broken;
> Wherefore of your sins you must be forsakers,
> If of Christ's death ye will be partakers.

His home was at Hartlebury, and he issued instructions
to his clergy each of them, "to obtain if possible a WHOLE

---

* Foxe, Townsend's Ed. iv., 642.
† Latimer to Cromwell, Sept. 4, 1535 ; Le Neve, *Fasti,* 298.
‡ *Acts and Monuments* (Townsend Ed.), vii., 461.

BIBLE, or at least a NEW TESTAMENT both in Latin and
English before Christmas." * "That each of you read
over and study every day one chapter at least." . . .
"That preaching be not laid aside for any manner of
observance, such as a procession or other ceremonies." In
Worcester cathedral he caused an image of the Virgin to be
stript of its ornaments and jewels. He was in his reforms
ably supported by HENRY (*Rand*) HOLBEACH, then the
prior. The image when stripped turned out to be the statue
of some bishop.

"Worcester is behind," writes Latimer, "an ancient
and poor city, and yet replenished by men of honesty,
though not most wealthy, for by reason of their 'lady'
[the image] they have been given to much idleness, but
now that she is gone, they may be turned to laboriousness,
and so from *ladyness* to godliness. But sir," continues
Latimer :—

> "This city is greatly charged with three things, their school,
> their bridge, and their wall. As for their school it hath been
> maintained heretofore by a brotherhood called a Gyld,† I trow,
> not without some guile, popishly pardoning, and therefore now
> worthily decried ; so that I am fain myself, poor as I am, to
> retain the schoolmaster there with my livery, meat and drink,
> upon the holiday, and some part of his living beside, because
> he is honest, and bringeth up their youth after the best sort.

* Strype, *Memorials*, (ed. 1822) I. ii., 368.
† The Guild of the Holy Trinity at Worcester, Nash, II. *App.* 138.

> Vouchsafe the two Friaries, Black and Grey, with their
> appurtenances, upon this poor ancient city to the maintenance of
> the aforesaid three things, so necessary for many good purposes,
> popishness changed into holiness, beggars unbeggared to avoid
> beggary, when lip-labouring of a few lewd friars should be
> turned into right praying of the whole city and town." *

Latimer was commissioned by the Crown to examine
the famous imposture of the Blood of Hales. It was a
noted relic kept in the Abbey of Hales in Gloucestershire,
said to be a portion of the Saviour's blood shed on Mount
Calvary for our salvation ; and the sight of it was supposed
to certify those who came and saw of their cleansing and
safety.   Latimer exposed the deception.   He writes :—

> " We have been bolting and shifting the blood of Hailes all
> this forenoon. It was wondrously and craftily enclosed and
> stopped up, for taking of care. And it cleaveth fast to the
> bottom of the glass that it is in. And verily it seemeth to be
> an unctious gum and compound of many things.
>
> We, Hugh, Bishop of Worcester, Henry, Prior of Worcester,
> Stephen, Abbot of Monastery of Hales, and Richard Tracy, Esq.,
> Oct. 28, 1538, repaired to the said monastery and have viewed
> a supposed relic called the blood of Hales enclosed within a
> round berall garnished in silver. It was opened before a
> multitude of people, and we found within, a little glass with
> gum, coloured like blood, honey clarified and coloured with
> saffron."

Latimer was very liberal in his diocese.   He writes :—

* These two friaries were accordingly granted to the bailiff and citizens of Worcester in
the following year.   Turner's *Notitia*, 626-27 ; London, 1744.

"I am more inclined to feed many grossly and neces-
sarily than a few deliciously and voluptuously. I delight
more to feed hungry bellies than to clothe dead walls." *

Among the Protestants whom Latimer appointed to help
in his diocese or to be his chaplains were Thomas Garrett
or Garrard, and Thomas Gybson, the printer. GARRARD
(born *circ.* 1500; died 1540), had been educated at *Corpus
Christi*, Oxford, and learned the truth of the Gospel from
the Holy Scriptures. Latimer had him as his chaplain at
Hartlebury in 1536.†

In Latimer's Register II., fol. 6*b*, Thomas Garrett is
named as incumbent of Hartlebury (1539), by Latimer's
appointment. He was a firm and consistent Protestant and
was compelled to carry a faggot in open procession from
St. Mary's to Friswide's, in Oxford. His accusation was,
"dispensing abroad works of Martin Luther, and teaching
the errors contained in them, namely, that we are justified
by faith only, and that every man may read and preach the
Word of God." ‡ He was burnt at Smithfield, 30 July, 1540.
THOMAS GYBSON graduated M.B. at Cambridge in 1511.
He wrote a Concordance to the New Testament, printed by
himself, and published in London, 1535. "This bringer,
Thomas Gybson, is a poor suitor to your lordship (Cromwell)

* 24 Dec. 1538, Hartlebury. Latimer to one in prison, Strype, *Memorials*, III., part ii.,
p. 296. Ed. of 1822.

† Latimer's *Life and Letters*, by Corrie, Parker Soc., II. 418.

‡ Foxe, *Acts and Mon.*, v. 421-428. Townsend's Ed.

that he may by your favour have the printing of our
book.   He is an honest, poor man, and will set it forth in
good letter and sell it cheap." *   He fled to Switzerland in
the reign of Mary, and was in Geneva in 1557.   He had
on his return a license to practise physic.   He taught the
Oxford clergyman, John Daye, printing, afterwards the
famous Protestant printer of Elizabeth's reign.   His wife and
daughter became members of the English congregation at
Geneva, 20 Nov., 1557.   He died in 1562.†   Thos. Gibson's
device was a sleeper awakened by one who points to the
rising sun.   Day adopted this device with the punning
motto, "Arise, for it is Day."

Latimer took the part of the poor against the oppression
and injustice of the rich.   He wrote a letter to Cromwell in
behalf of a minister named Large, "who was wronged by
one Mr. Clopton, a papist commissioner.   This Clopton
had never heard Large, nor could (if he had) have judged of
his doctrine, yet he stirred up the people against him as
Master Nevell can tell you." ‡   Latimer looked after the
remote parts of his diocese.   "Persuade Anthony Barker
(of Stratford-on-Avon), to tarry and preach there, to the
reformation of that blind end of my diocese." §   Dr. Barnes
hath preached here with me at Hartlebury, and at my

* Latimer's *Life*, by Corrie, II. 380.
† *Dict. Nat. Biog.*, Cooper, *Athenæ Cantab.*, I. 217, 553.
‡ From Pershore, in his visitation, 6 Oct., 1537.
§ Latimer's *Works*, Corrie (Parker Soc.) II. 384.

request at Winchester and Evesham. He is alone in handling a piece of Scripture, and in setting forth Christ he hath no fellow." *

But Latimer's influence was most telling in the steps he took for BIBLE READING and BIBLE CIRCULATION. He had as chaplain RODOLPH BRADFORD,† who had been imprisoned two years in Ireland as a hawker of Frith's English Testaments, and for preaching the Gospel. And he prepared the way to bring as a resident in Worcester, the printer JOHN OSWEN from Ipswich, appointed by Edward VI. "prynter for the Principality of Wales, and marshes of the same." In the British Museum are three NEW TESTAMENTS in English printed by OSWEN in WORCESTER, one small folio, 1548; one quarto, 1550; and one a pocket Testament 16mo. To Worcester belongs the honourable distinction of being the first English city outside London in which at this early date English Bibles were printed for the use of the people. And beautiful specimens of Black-letter printing they are, well worth a visit to the British Museum Library to see. That JOHN OSWEN was himself a zealous Protestant is clear from his address "*The Printer to the Reader,*" prefixed to one of his New Testaments. He says : "Whereas some Testaments have had notes at the end of the chapters, I have added notes, but not in the margin, or there would not

---

* *Ibid.* p. 389.

† Born at Twyford in Oxfordshire, educated at Eton, at King's, Camb. 1519., D.D in 1535.

be room for noting other places of Scripture. The best means to understand Scripture is to turn to other places making mention of the same thing. Also the unlearned might read the notes as if they were Scripture. So I put them at the end of the book. Here is an Almanack at what time the sun rises and sets through every month of the year, and what Lesson in the New Testament is read at Matins and Evensong.

Imprinted the xii
daye of January,
Anno do. M. CCCCC. L.
at Worcester by
JOHN OSWEN." *

The following are specimens of the notes :—

Close of Prologue to the Romans. Now go to Reader, and according to the order of Paul's writing even so be thou. 1. Behold thyself diligently in the law of God, and see there thy just damnation. 2. Turn thine eyes to Christ, and see there the exceeding mercy of thy most kind and loving Father. 3. Remember that Christ made not his Atonement that thou shouldest anger God again, neither died He for thy sins that thou shouldest live still in them. Neither cleanseth He thee that thou shouldest return as a swyne unto thine own puddle again ; but that thou shouldest be a new creature and live a new lyfe after the will of God, and not of the flesh. And be diligent, lest through thine own negligence and unthankfulness thou lose this favour and mercy again. Farewell. †

---

* *See* Oswen's *New Test. Preface*, Brit. Mus. Lib.
† John Oswen's *New Testament*, 1548, 16mo., B. M. Lib.

"JESUS, or after the Hebrew *Jesua*, is by interpretation SAVIOUR. CHRIST, in Hebrew MESSIAS, signifies *anointed*. EMANUEL is interpreted *God with us*, which name was given unto Christ because He, being God, was (as Paul witnesseth) found like unto us in all things, sin only excepted."

"When Paul says ' Faith justifieth,' understand thereby faith causeth that we be accounted just, reputed righteous, and that our sins be not imputed to us, but forgiven for Christ's sake. When James saith, 'works justify,' he means this :—Works declare us just, and show evidently that we be righteous.— Thus thou shall make them accord." *

Soon after the passing of the *Act of the Six Articles*, Latimer resigned his bishopric, 1 July, 1539, and when he first put off his rochet in his chamber among his friends, suddenly he gave a skip on the floor for joy, feeling his shoulder so light, and being discharged, as he said, of such a heavy burden.† Although the House of Commons, 9 Jan., 1548-9, desired that Latimer might be reinstated in the see of Worcester, he peremptorily refused to accept that or any other bishopric. On the accession of Queen Mary, he was committed to the Tower, and on 16 October, 1555, was burnt to death with Bishop Ridley at Canditch near the front of Balliol College, Oxford. In the flames he addressed to Ridley the memorable words, " Be of good comfort, master Ridley, and play the man : we shall this

---

* *Ibid.* Note on the Epistle of James.
† Foxe, *Acts and Monuments*, as before, vii. 463.

day by God's grace light such a candle in England, as I
trust, shall never be put out." *

It is true that the principle of religious equality was
not fully understood by any religious party in Latimer's
day; but the statement that he cruelly preached at and
taunted a Romanist before his sufferings will not bear
investigation.   The Romanist to be executed was Forest,
whom Burnet † describes as "an indifferent kind of person;"
and there is a letter extant from Latimer to Lord Cromwell,
saying "Sir, if it be your wish as it is, that I shall *play the
fool* after my customable manner when Forest shall suffer,
I would wish that my stage stood near unto Forest, for I
would endeavour myself so to content the people, that
therewith I might also convert Forest, God so helping, or
rather altogether working; wherefore I would that he
should hear what I shall say."   Latimer considered the
duty so distasteful that he calls it "playing the fool;" yet
he desires, seeing the King ordered him do it, that the
preaching might be blest to the conversion of the man.
We have not the very words preached, but this expression
of his intention frees Latimer from the accusation of wanton
taunt and cruelty on the occasion.‡

---

* His dress was noteworthy when on his trial. "He had a kerchief on his head, and
upon it a nightcap or two, and a great cap (such as townsmen use, with two broad flaps to
button under the chin), wearing an old threadbare Bristowe frieze gown girded to his body
with a penny leather girdle, at the which hanged, by a long string of leather, his Testament; and his spectacles without case, depending about his neck upon his breast." Thus
he appeared before his judges. Foxe, as before, vii. 529.

† *History of the Reformation*, IV., 432.

‡ *Remains of Latimer*, Corrie (Parker Soc.), I. 266, II., 391-2.

It must be remembered also that the executions of Papists were few and far between, and on political grounds; whereas those of Protestants were wholesale in Mary's reign, and in accordance with the doctrine of Romanism, still avowed in the Syllabus and Vatican Decrees.*

In proof of the firm hold which the teachings of Latimer, and the reading of Holy Scripture had taken upon the families of Worcester, and even upon the young, we cite the following narrative:— †

> In 1546, JOHN DAVIS a boy of twelve years, pupil in the Grammar School, was apprentice or servant in the house of Mr. Thomas Johnson, Apothecary in Worcester, his own uncle, who used to read the New Testament and other good English books, and composed a Ballad on "the Shaven Crowns." John learnt himself to read these books and imbibed their teachings; but his mistress, Alice Johnson the Apothecary's wife, made complaint, and at the suggestion of certain of the Canons and one Thos. Parton, and the wife of Nicholas Brooke, organ maker, planned a way to betray the boy. They employed a schoolfellow (Oliver Brooke), under pretence to be instructed, to see his English books and to get hold of some of his writings against *the Six Articles*. The boy was siezed and imprisoned; one Richard Howborough held his finger in the candle to persuade him from burning, and frighten him to recant. But John was firm, and was removed to an inner prison called the Peep-hole, "where Robert Yould the bailiff

* *Syllabus*, Dec. 8, 1864, § V 24; § X.

† The Imprisonment of John Davis, a boy of Worcester. Written by himself in after life. MS. Harl. 425, fol. 69. *See* Camden Society, Nichols, J. G.

laid upon him a pair of bolts, so that he could not lift up his
small legs, but slipt them forward upon the ground, the coldness
of which irons he felt in his ancles all his life." With these
bolts fastened to him he had to lie night after night on the cold
ground. His relatives were not allowed to see him ; but two
Canons came to see if he would recant. He was brought
before the bishop's chancellor in the Worcester Guildhall.
Being found guilty he was sent back to the common gaol,
among thieves and murderers, to await execution. But by the
mercy of God he was rescued, before the sentence was finally
pronounced Henry VIII. died, and Edward VI. came to the
throne. This steadfast boy endured in prison from August 14
till within seven days of Easter. In Mary's reign he had to
leave the country. He lived to grow to riper years and became
a minister of Christ's Gospel.*

Let us hope that many an English boy or girl taught in
our English Board Schools, without priest or catechism, to
read those HOLY SCRIPTURES, "that are able to make wise
unto salvation," in these days of semi-Romish churchism,
will be firm to witness for Christ and His gospel in riper
years, should the Whitgift and Aylmer of 1897 succeed
in setting aside the BIBLE for clerical-indoctrination and
church-superstitions in old England again.

The other martyr Bishop whose life and death honour
the see of Worcester and sowed the seeds of Protestant
Nonconformity in the city and county was JOHN HOOPER.
Born in Somerset, he graduated B.A. at Oxford in 1519,

---

* Foxe, *Acts and Monuments*, Townsend's Ed., viii., 554.

JOHN HOOPER.
Martyr Bishop of Worcester.

HUGH LATIMER.
Martyr Bishop of Worcester.

and embracing the tenets of Martin Luther, was as a
preacher of Christ's Gospel compelled to flee once and
again from the inquisitorial persecution of ecclesiastics in
England.   In 1546 he found refuge in Switzerland.   He
married Anna de Tserelas, a lady of Antwerp, at Basle, in
1546.   He settled in Zurich, and enjoyed the warm friendship of Bullinger, whose love of Holy Scripture he imbibed,
and followed Zwingli and John Laski * in his views of the
simplicity of Christ's church and its organization.   Hooper
returned to England in 1549, and became chaplain to the
Protector Somerset.   In 1550 he refused the bishopric of
Gloucester, because he would not wear the vestments, which
he regarded as impious, and opposed to Scripture.
Edward VI. with his own hand erased the obnoxious
requirement, and issued a dispensation freeing him from
any pains and penalties incurred by a departure from the
forms of consecration.   Nevertheless, the clerical party
succeeded in imprisoning him for a time.   By the advice of
Bucer he was consecrated March 8, 1550, without the vestments ; by compromise he was to wear them only when he
preached before the king.   In a letter to Bullinger, dated
June 29, 1550, Hooper says, that at Easter the king offered
him the bishopric of Gloucester.†   The first offer was it
appears the see of WORCESTER, that of Gloucester being

* LASKI (1499-1560) a Reformer born at Lask in Poland, friend of Erasmus and Latimer,
intimate with Edward VI., *Dictionary of National Biography*.

† Hooper's *Remains*, II. 434 (Parker Society).

C

suppressed, and made an archdeaconry to Worcester. Then objections being raised to this suppression, both sees were united like Bath and Wells, and Hooper was designated " bishop of Gloucester and Worcester " in 1552.* The fact is, Hooper was consecrated by proxy in 1550–1. Moreover, the Earl of Warwick's letter on behalf of Hooper, there designated " my lord elect of Gloucester," is dated 23 July, 1550.† And in an old record by Nash (Appendix 97) we find this entry :—1551, June 21, Bishop Hooper came to town (Worcester) with his wife and daughter ; he had a long beard ; and in all his time were no children confirmed. August 12. The high altar was taken down to the ground, all the quire with the Bishop's throne taken down.‡ Edward VI. in his letter of appointment names as Hooper's great qualification " his singular learning in the Holy Scriptures, and his unblameable morals." §

" Master Hooper," says Foxe, " entering his diocese, did there employ his time which the Lord lent him under King Edward's reign, with diligence. So careful was he to train up the flock of Christ in the true word of salvation, in both dioceses. No father in his family, no gardener in his garden, nor husbandman in his vineyard was more

* See the *Carta Originales* given by Thomas, *Bishops of Worcester*, Appendix No. 138. pp. 165 *sqq.*

† Foxe, *Acts and Monuments*, Townsend's Ed., vi. 641.

‡ *Collecta in cust.* Dan. Hughes ; Edgar Tower, Worcester.

§ Thomas (as before) p. 208, Appendix No. 138, p. 165.

or better occupied than he among his flock, going about
the towns and villages teaching and preaching to the
people. Twice I was, as I remember, in his house at Worcester, where, in his common hall, I saw a table spread
with good store of meat, and beset full of beggars and poor
folk : and I, asking his servants what this meant, they told
me that every day their master's manner was to have to
dinner a certain number of poor folk of the said city by
course, who were served by four at a mess with hot and
wholesome meats ; and when they were served, then he
himself sat down to dinner, and not before. After this sort
and manner Master Hooper executed the office of a most
careful and vigilant pastor, so long as the state of religion
in King Edward's time did safely flourish." *

Hooper had a valuable helper in his Christlike work in
Oswen, the printer of Worcester, and there is extant a small
16mo. volume, a comment on Romans xiii., entitled :—

> "Godly and Necessary Annotations on the xiii. chapter to
> the Romans, set forth by the right vigilant Pastor, John
> Hoper, 1551."

In his prefatory letter "to my very loving and dere-
beloved fellow-labourers in the Word of God, William
Jenkyns, dean of the Cathedral, and John Williams, doctor
in laws" :

> "Read unto the people every Saturday and Sunday this 13th
> chapter as I have set it forth, because of the greater offenses and

---

* Foxe, *Acts and Monuments*, Townsend Ed., Vol. vi., 644.

sins of the richer sort of people and also of the poor both in this shire
and others.   The rich man so encroacheth, gathereth together,
and obtaineth so much into his own hands, that he alone
possesseth the earth and liveth thereby, and his poor neighbour
is ready to die for lack ; so that he is brought into Tantalus'
pain.   Meat and drink, cattle and corn enough on every side of
him, yet he may rather die for lack than the insatiable and
never contented covetous persons will price their goods so as
poor men, their wives and their children, may be able to buy
reasonable pennyworths of God's abundant plenty and riches
that He bringeth out of the earth.

I require you most diligently to teach them this chapter every
week ; one part of it the Saturday at evensong ; the other at
morning prayer, and the third part, the Sunday at evensong.

Yours with all my heart,

brother and fellow preacher,

JOHN, GLOUCESTER."

*" It is Jesus Christ, the Son of God, most dearly beloved, and
in whom the Father is contented, and by whom he is reconciled
unto all sinners that repent and believe His promises, for the
merits and shedding of Christ's blood, His dearly beloved Son."*

A copy of Bishop Hooper's *Visitation Book* for his
double diocese of Gloucester and Worcester lies among the
Morrice MSS. in Dr. Williams's Library, and the following
are among the injunctions named :—

That none teach any thing necessary for the salvation of man
other than that contained in the Book of God's Holy Word,
called the Old and New Testament.

That they teach the justification of man only by the faith of Jesus Christ ; not by the merit of any man's good works.

The doctrine of Purgatory, Prayers for the Dead, veneration, invocating, worshipping of saints and images, is contrary and injurious to the honour of Christ, our only Mediator and Redeemer.

In the sacrament of the Lord's Supper there is no transubstantiation, no corporal or local presence of Christ in, under, or with the bread and wine ; but [it is to be partaken] spiritually by faith, believing the Son of God to be made man, and that by His death He might satisfy for the sins of the world.

Among his injunctions (1551) to the clergy are the following :—

That every one of you preach every Sunday.

Be diligent in reading and studying the Holy Scriptures.

Teach the Ten Commandments as they stand in Exodus xx. and no otherwise.*

Remove all images and signs of superstition from the church.†

* It is well known that Romanists omit the second commandment, and make the number up to ten by dividing the Tenth Commandment into two.

† This had already been done in Worcester. " 1547 and S.   The great brazen candlestick and beam of timber before the High Altar was taken away.   10 Jan.   So were all the Images on the High Altar, and on all the church, destroyed.   No candles hallowed or borne on Candlemas day.   No Ashes hallowed on Allhallow day.   No Palms hallowed nor ✠ borne on Palm Sunday.   No creeping to the ✠ on Good Friday.   No fire hallowed but the Pascal Taper and the Font, on Easter eve.   On Easter Day at the Resurrection, the Pix with the Sacrament in it was taken out of the sepulchre, the Quire singing *Christ is Risen*, without procession.

20 Oct.   The Cup with the Body of Christ was taken from the High Altar in the Cathedral and so it was in other churches and chapels 1549.   On Good Friday no sepulchre set up.   On Easter Eve no paschal hallowed, nor censer, nor font; and on Easter Tuesday, April 23, the mass, mattins, and evensong, said and sung in ENGLISH.

1549.   All Mass-books, Graduals, Grailes, Pies, Portuasses, Legends, brought to the Bishop of the see and burnt." *Collecta in cust.*   Dan. Hughes, Edgar Tower, Worcester. From Bp. Blandford's Diary.

No man in the parish that use to keep open any ale-house, tavern, tap-house, is to do so at the time of service, before noon or after noon.

No glass painting of any image or picture of any saint in the windows.

That ye cause to be defaced all such images as do yet remain painted upon any of the walls of your churches.

That there be provided in every church a Bible of the largest volume in English, and the Paraphrase of Erasmus in a box.

And among the enquiries for the people are the following :—

Whether the Table for the Communion be decked and apparelled behind and before as altars were wont to be decked.

Whether the table stand in such a place as the people may most conveniently hear the godly psalm and prayers said by the minister at the time of service and the Communion.

Whether there be a Bible of largest volume with the Paraphrase of Erasmus in English, in a convenient place in the church ; so that everybody may come to the same at time convenient.

Whether all images are taken clean out of the church.

Whether the clergy require any to come to auricular confession.

Regarding the effect of these articles in his Worcester diocese, Hooper writes on July 6, 1552. "Since my coming down I have been to Worcester, and thought not to have departed thence till I had set things in good order as near as I could. But the negligence of the ministers in Gloucestershire compelled me to return." He came back to Worcester soon, bringing with him the same articles, which

led him into controversy with two of the canons of the
Cathedral, Henry Joliffe and Robert Johnson, who objected
to sign. Mr. Cheke and Mr. Hurley were on the bishop's
side. "I dare say," he writes, "there is not a church to
preach God's word in more goodly within this realm, but I
see much mischief in men's hearts by many tokens." He
was untiring in his ministerial labours, preaching every
day, and occasionally three times a day. "I entreat you,"
writes his wife to Bullinger (Apr. 3, 1551), "to recommend
him to be more moderate in his labours, for he preaches
four, or at least three times every day." The lives of his
family as well as his own were placed in jeopardy by the
sweating sickness, a fatal disorder then prevalent. On the
death of Edward VI. (6 July, 1553), and the accession of
Mary, he was summoned under the sway of Romanism to
Richmond, and imprisoned in the Fleet; and after many
persecutions and privations he was burnt to death at
Gloucester, on Feb. 9, 1554–5. He walked cheerfully to
the fatal spot, and there knelt down and prayed thus :—

> "O Lord Jesus, for whose love I leave willingly this life, and
> desire the bitter death of the cross with the loss of all my
> worldly things, Thou seest that when I might live in wealth to
> worship a false God, I choose rather the torments of my body
> and the loss of this my life, and have counted all but vile dust
> that I might win Thee. Such love, dear Lord, hast Thou laid
> up in my breast that I hunger for Thee as the deer that is
> wounded desireth the soil; so send Thy Holy Comforter to
> aid and strengthen this weak piece of earth, that I may pass

through the fury of this fire into Thy bosom. O Heavenly
Father forgive me my sins as I forgive all the world. O sweet
Son of God my Saviour, spread Thy wings over me." His last
words were, "Lord Jesus have mercy upon me; Lord Jesus
receive my spirit." *

It is evident that our history would be lacking in its
very foundations, had we omitted the lives of these two
nonconforming bishops of Worcester, who by their teaching
and in their martyrdom sowed the seeds of Protestantism—
and "kindled such a candle in England as by God's grace
shall never be put out." To them we owe an open Bible,
a simple communion-table, a plain gospel preached in England, an abhorrence of Ritualism and Sacerdotalism, whether
Anglican or Roman; and the distinctive features of our
British Christianity, Welsh, Scotch, and English. Our
watchword is, as Chillingworth put it, THE BIBLE
ONLY. Nothing so clearly indicates the Romish *Geist*
now influencing many priests and prelates of the Establishment, as does their present outcry against our Board-schools,
—"ONLY the Bible in them." After three centuries our
eyes behold the two Hierarchies, Roman and Anglican,
warring side by side, and with one voice, against the Bible
ONLY—against the sufficiency of Holy Scripture in the hands
of the people. For them Latimer and Hooper suffered
in vain. Protestants may have the conflict of the Reformation over again, but victory must again be on our side.
The Nonconformist plea is demonstrated; Reformation in

* Bishop Hooper's *Works*, Parker Society, Biog. notice, vol. II. xxix.

the seventeenth century did not go far enough. Next time it will be more complete, Hebrews iv. 12.

I searched in vain for any wills of Latimer and Hooper in the Prerogative court. Whatever little they possessed was confiscated. They gave up all for CHRIST.

Staying at St. Leonards-on-Sea while writing this, I visited three churches of the English Establishment. In the *first*, Purgatory was preached by a priest dressed up in scarlet like the Pope, a great cross carried before him by a stalwart youth in red ; processions, bowings to the altar, crossings, &c. In a *second*, similar bowings and crossings, lighted candles on the altar, behind which was a painting, and above in the window the body of Christ on the cross ; banners borne in procession about the aisles ; and this admonition in a small book in the pew :—" Fix your mind on the great fact that you are present at the SACRIFICE ; notice when the Consecration takes place, so that you may not let our Lord's Sacramental Advent pass without doing homage to Him as He VISITS THE ALTAR in His humility." In a *third*, the Romish Mass was transacted ; gorgeously apparelled priests, mimicking to the letter the genuflections and posturings of that church, which simply scorns their Orders and condemns them as lay-schismatics. Prayers were gabbled over like the Latin of the Missal, incense in clouds, grovelling prostrations before the host, elevation of the host ; the elements not given to the congregation ; in fact all the idolatry which their own prayer book designates as " blasphemous fables and dangerous deceits." This spectacle is transacted week by week and year after year beneath the eyes of the bishop who either approves or connives. And this is the religion practiced with impunity in the church which Protestant England is paying for and patronizing by law.

III.

The Puritan Lecturers.

URING the Marian persecution, many Protestant ministers fled to Germany and Switzerland, and found a home in the Reformed churches of the Continent. Among these was EDWIN SANDYS.* He went to Strasburg for a year, and thence to Peter Martyr's house in Zurich. He returned to England on Jan. 13, 1558–9, and was made Bishop of Worcester, 21 Dec. 1559, and one of the translators of the Bishops' Bible, 1565. He continued at Worcester till 1570. Edwin Sandys was disposed to favour the Puritans, and rebuked Queen Elizabeth for having a crucifix. He had for his chaplain at Worcester,† Thomas Wilson,‡ who had found a refuge at Frankfort. Returning in 1559, he was

---

* Born 1519 at Hawkshead, Furness, Lancashire; B.A. of St. John's, Cambridge, 1539, and afterwards Vice-chancellor of the University. See Cooper's *Athenæ Cantab.*, II., 25.

† Neal, *Hist. of the Puritans*, I., 132, 160.

‡ Born in Westmoreland, fellow of St. John's, Camb., 1548.

ordained and made a canon of Worcester. In the Convocation of 1562-3, he with Robert Avys, served as proctor for the Chapter of Worcester, and voted (as did Bishop Sandys), against the habits, the cross in Baptism, kneeling at the Communion, the minister turning his back to the people, and other ceremonies which the Puritans objected to as Romanistic.* He afterwards became Dean of Worcester, and vicar of Blockley. His predecessor in the Deanery, Dean Pedder, also gave his vote against the habits and other ceremonies. Indeed, among those present there was a majority (43 against 37) on the Puritan side; but by means of proxies the motion was negatived by a majority of one. Wilson and Avys, representing Worcester, also signed certain articles demanding, " that all images of the Trinity and of the Holy Ghost be defaced, and that roods and all other images that have been, or hereafter may be superstitiously abused, be taken away out of all places, public and private, and utterly destroyed." †

Another Puritan preacher and lecturer in Worcester was ROBERT ABBOT, elder brother of Archbishop Abbot. He had been educated at Guildford, his birthplace,‡ and was scholar of Balliol College, Oxford, in 1575. He became rector of All Saints, in Worcester, in 1588. A sermon he

* Strype, *Annals*, I. i., 264, 502. Neal, I. 150.
† Strype, *Annals*, I. i., 508, 512.
‡ Fuller's *Worthies*, Surrey. Abbot married Bridget Cheynell, mother of the eminent Presbyterian divine, Francis Cheynell, *Dict. of Nat. Biog.*

preached at Worcester resulted in his appointment to lecture in the Cathedral on Sunday afternoons. Large congregations gathered in the Nave, and listened to his Bible preaching, and his denunciations of Romanising tendencies. A work of his is extant entitled, *" The Mirror of Papists' Subtleties;* discovering divers wretched and miserable evasions and shifts gathered in behalf of one Paul Spence, late prisoner *in the Castle of Worcester,* but now living at his liberty abroad."* He tells us he published this book only for the citizens of Worcester, and people thereabouts, for their satisfaction in this cause, wherein he knew many of them desired to be satisfied. This was Robert Abbot's first-fruits, being a young man of thirty, and in the spring of 1590.†

In the same year (1589-90) the Worcester corporation appointed a Lecturer "to preach at the College [as the Cathedral was then called] every Sunday, so long as it seems good to this house." The Lecturer was MR. KINNETT,‡ and he continued to fill the office till his death. He was succeeded by MR. HARKELL,§ and in 1627 the corporation petitioned Charles I. for a prebend for the Lecturer, who received a portion of his income from them, which should have been supplemented by a grant from the Dean and Chapter. In 1619 the king issued an order—(1) That the

* Strype, *Life of Whitgift,* II. pp. 210, 211.

† Robert Abbot afterwards became professor of divinity in Oxford, and Bishop of Salisbury. See Strype as before, and *Dict. of National Biog.*

‡ Noake's *Monastery and Cathedral of Worcester,* p. 551.

§ Noake, *Worcester in olden times,* p. 114.

Sunday afternoon sermon be in the form of question and answer. (2) That every Lecturer read divine service according to the Liturgy, in his surplice and hood, before the lecture. (3) That where a Lecture is set up it may be read by a company of grave and orthodox Divines, near adjoining and in the same diocese, and that they preach in gowns, not in cloaks as too many do use. (4) That if a corporation do maintain a single Lecturer, he be not suffered to preach till he professes his willingness to take upon him a living with cure of souls within that incorporation ; and that he do actually take such benefice or cure as soon as it shall be fairly procured for him.* Under this order Archbishop Laud endeavoured to suppress and silence the Lecturers ; and the Bishop of Worcester certifies to him that " he is less troubled with Nonconformists since Mr. Wheatley, of Banbury, gave over his lecture at Stratford, and during this heavy visitation at Worcester he hath caused the Lectures to cease." In 1635 Roger Mainwaring † gives Laud an account of what he had done in the cathedral.

> "1. An altar of stone or marble erected. 2. The wall
> behind the altar covered with azure-coloured stuff and white
> silk lace. 3. The altar adorned with a pall. 4. A rail erected
> from one side of the choir to the other to fence the holy table." ‡

In 1636-7, March 13, the king writes to the mayor and

---

* Document in Edgar Tower, Worc. Given by Noake, *Cath. of Worc.*, p. 552.

† Mainwaring, the notorious preacher of the King's prerogative to levy taxes apart from Parliament, *Dict. of Nat. Biog.*

‡ S. P. O. *Dom.* Charles I., 1635, Sept. 24.

chief officers of Worcester :—" He hears that the service in
the choir of the cathedral is very much neglected, and almost
utterly deserted by all that are of the best rank in the city.
The king enjoins the mayor and corporation to attend on
all Sundays, morning and evening. This royal injunction
to be entered among the acts of the city." *

From these documents it is clear that the people of
Worcester resisted the Romanizing tendencies of Laud and
Bishop Mainwaring, and were determined to have their
Protestant preaching, and their Lecturers. Accordingly
we find the following Petitions :—

> 1636 7, March 13. Petition of the Mayor, Alderman and
> Citizens of Worcester to Archbishop Laud. " Within the city
> of Worcester there are nine parishes, whereof many of the
> incumbents are NOT preaching ministers ; whereby a great many
> of his Majesty's subjects are not so well instructed in the WORD
> OF GOD as they ought to have been. For remedy whereof the
> citizens at their charge for many years past made choice of a
> LEARNED PREACHER in the cathedral, to preach every Sunday,
> after evening prayer done in the parish churches, and before
> evening service in the cathedral ; there being no parish church
> sufficient to contain half the company that resorted thereunto.
> They would willingly continue, but are restrained by Mr. Dean.†

Again, S.P.O. *Dom.* Ch. I., 1639, Nov. 8:—

> " Petition of DANIEL TYAS, mayor, and citizens of Worcester
> to Archbishop Laud. There has been time out of mind in the
> west end of the Cathedral Church of Worcester an ancient

---

* S. P. O. *Dom.*   Charles I. 1636-7, March 13.
† S. P. O.   Vol. 349.   Case D. Car. I., No. 12.

pulpit for daily prayers and preaching of the Word of God with convenient seats and kneelings for the citizens and others ; to which place very great numbers are wont to resort, it being a very populous city. In 1637 your Grace, as it is informed, ordered that all those seats should be removed, the pulpit taken down and removed with moveable seats to the west end of the choir. Owing to the unevenness of this place, which was the belfry, with many doors near the same, it was found very unwholesome for the auditory, especially in winter time, so that the preaching hath been removed into the choir. Now the choir is very unfit, not being capable to receive a sixth part of the auditory, and other ways very inconvenient. It is apparent since the removal thither, by reason of the extraordinary thronging, and uneasiness of continual standing both of men and women, to the great hazard of their health, for want of convenient seats, by which means the ancient men and women are constrained to forbear coming thither, with many hundreds more who cannot come nor be contained in that place ; by which means to our great grief both church, prayers, and preaching are much neglected, and thereby God much dishonoured. We pray that the said pulpit may be restored to its former situation at the west end of the Cathedral, its ancient place, and where there is no door for passage, but only a dead wall, against which the Mayor and his Brethren sat with their backs to it, that thereby the full auditory of this populous city may comfortably meet together for conveniently hearing the Word of God, and so much the rather for that we are informed that the end of the church was enlarged for that purpose by an ancient Bishop of the See."

Underwritten.—" Bishop Thornborough, Bishop of Worcester, together with the prebendaries undernamed do join in this petition."

Endorsed by Archb. Laud, "with Dr. Potter's answer."*

Nov. 18, 1639, Dr. Christopher Potter, the Dean (who had been a Puritan,† but had become Laud's creature), writes :—

> "The senators and their wives sat there in pomp and more state than at their guildhall. They were erected in Dean Hall's time, who was the engineer to contrive them in that form. On Sunday mornings before sermon during choral service some walked and talked in the nave; others gathered their auditors about them in the seats, and read to them some English divinity so loudly, as that the singers in the choir were much disturbed by them, all despising that service. When the seats were taken down the citizens fly to their oracle and asylum, the old bishop (of late feeble, now lusty), who has indeed debauched that people by his popular fawning and flattering them in all their fancies. . . . The complying of our weak silly bishop and these silly weak ones of my company (I except Dr. Smith), has put them into such a fury and malice against me, Mr. Broughton, and Mr. Tomkins. They take this for a persecution of the gospel, and us to be the authors of it, and you too, as far as they dare. The times are crazy, and I hope your wisdom and goodness may for peace and quietness yield a little to their folly. Gratify them with their own beloved place, till that mistress of fools, their own experience, shew them the vanity of their desires." ‡

Dec. 30, 1639.   Dr. Christ. Potter to Archb. Laud.

> "From Worcester I hear our citizens are highly displeased.

---

* *Calendar of State Papers, Dom.*, Ch. I., 1639, Vov. 8; pp. 79, 80.

† Ch. Potter had a Lectureship at Abingdon, where he was much resorted to for his edifying way of preaching.

‡ S. P. O. *Dom.*, Ch. I., 1639. *Calendar of S. P.*, 1639, pp. 107-8.

Though the King granted their petition, their sermon place at
the west end and decent seats, he granted not their high and
lofty seats. The ruins of these remain with us, and are not
worth twopence to us ; and they may make the best use of them
for new seats, if they please. . . If you think meet, they may be
gratified by permitting their Lecturer HALSETER, an honest
harmless man, as I hear, to preach there on Sundays after
evening service, no church in the city being able to receive
their multitude."

This correspondence illustrates what is known of the
interference of Archb. Laud all over the country with
Charles I.'s power and influence at his back, and the
strong firm Protestantism of the people, who will have the
Gospel and the Preachers, and not the ceremonies and the
priests. As to HALSETER here named by Dean Potter, he
became during the Commonwealth minister of Thorley in
Hertfordshire, where he is described as " John Halseter,
M.A., a godly, learned and orthodox divine."[*] We find
also Thomas Halseter as one of the Assistant Commissioners and Triers for Herts [†] in 1654. But with reference
to him in Worcester the following letter of Charles I. gives
a different estimate of him.

"Jan. 21, 1642. We are informed that JOHN HALCISTER,
parson of St. Nicholas, and Henry Hacket, parson of St.
Helen's, in the county of Worcester, have long continued to be
very schismatical and seditious preachers, and that having

[*] *Commons' Journals* III. March 7, 1642-3.
[†] See my *Nonc. in Herts*, pp. 709, 834.

abandoned their said cures, they are now actually joined the rebels." *

Among the same letters from the king we find one to Prideaux, the Bishop of Worcester, warning him against Brownists, Anabaptists and other Sectaries. It is dated 22 Dec. 1642.

> "Charles Rex. Rev. Father in God, as often as we observe the distracted and calamitous condition of our whole kingdom, occasioned by the present rebellion, we cannot but notice, that a principal cause of the said rebellion have [sic] been the great increase of Brownists, Anabaptists, and other Sectaries and persons mistaken and mispersuaded in their religion. And therefore for the remedying and preventing of anything of that nature that may be amiss in your Sea, and for putting in execution of our Ecclesiastical lawes which lately have been almost neglected, Our will and pleasure is, and we do hereby strictly require you with all care and vigilance to attend your pastoral charge ; and to that end to reside at our city of Worcester, for the better taking account of such Acts and things as belong to your office and jurisdiction."

The issue of this letter as far as the bishop Prideaux is concerned appears in the following :—

> "1642, Dec. 12, for ringing a peale upon my lord bishop's return to Worcester, after eleven weeks' absence, since first the rebels entered Worcester," 2s. 6d.

As to the demands of the Mayor and Citizens for their service in the Cathedral it appears they gained their point,

---

* Bundle of Letters of Charles I. in the custody of the Dean and Chapter of Worcester, in the Chapter House. HENRY HACKET, B.A., was appointed incumbent of Elmley Castle in 1633, and came to St. Helen's, Worcester, in 1636. *See* Nash's *Worcestershire*.

and the Dean and Chapter, in spite of Laud and Charles I., had to yield, as the following letter shows :—

> " Sir, We have treated with the Mayor and Sheriffs and some of the special citizens about their petition against the D. and C., and do find them somewhat inclinable to peace. The terms, we gather, they will stand to, are :—
>
> The having their seats and the pulpit made as formerly they were. £20 *per an.* towards their Lecturer's stipend. The School to be reduced to the old place. Their freedom of Burial in the Church and Churchyard at the old rates. The weekly alms to be given to their poor as heretofore. That the offended Bishop may have satisfaction and his consent obtained to a peace and retraction of the petition, and that Mr. Tompkins the sub-dean (with whom they seem to be highly offended) must submit. Dated 1 Apr., 1641."*

Among the occasional Lecturers was the devout and learned HENRY BRIGHT, of Balliol College, Oxford. He took his M.A. Jan. 27, 1586-7. He was a native of Worcester, and became Master of the King's school in the city, a post which he filled for 35 years (1591–1626) with great efficiency. He had a most excellent faculty in instructing youths in Latin, Greek, and Hebrew, and most of his pupils distinguished themselves at the Universities. For the last seven years of his life he was prebendary of the Cathedral (fifth stall). He was an excellent preacher, resorted to far and near. He died March 4, 1626, and was

* MS. in Edgar Tower.

buried in the Cathedral." *   Fuller writes, "I beheld Master Bright placed by Divine Providence in this city in the Marches that he might equally communicate the lustre of grammar learning to youth both of England and Wales." Joseph Hall, Dean of Worcester at the time, wrote Bright's epitaph, which Fuller gives. †

* Wood's *Fasti*, II. 132.
† *Worthies of England*, Tegg's Ed. III., 376.

THE REV. RICHARD BAXTER,
Born 1615, Died 1691.
Minister of Kidderminster, 1641 1662.

IV.

The Commonwealth Ministers.

In the summer of the year 1636 a young man of twenty-three years, delicate in looks and of weakly frame, visited Worcester to receive ordination at the hands of the old bishop, John Thornborough, now in his 90th year. The youth had never been to college; but he was a good scholar; and his application was backed up by Richard Foley, sometime mayor of Dudley, who had lately founded a grammar school in that borough, and had been advised to the appointment of this young man as master. His examination being satisfactorily passed, the old bishop ordained, with other candidates, the young schoolmaster,[*]

---

[*] Baxter did not take *imposition of hands* to be absolutely essential to ordination. He mentions "a bishop of Worcester in his time, so lame of the gout that he could not move his hand to a man's head, and yet never heard a nullity suspected in his ordinations." Calamy's *Abridgment*, i., 134. The bishop referred to must have been John Thornborough, who was a martyr to the gout, and as we have said, 90 years of age when he ordained Baxter. Those ordained on the occasion probably had no bishop's hand on their heads.

and he became a clergyman of the Established Church.
That young man was RICHARD BAXTER, a name more
widely known and honoured than that of the prelate who
set him apart to the work of teaching and ministration.
Little did the aged prelate think that the obscure, weakly,
young schoolmaster before him was to become the leader
of the Nonconformists of England, and one of the most
voluminous and distinguished writers of the century.
Baxter teaching scholars at Dudley, after a short ministry
at Bridgenorth as assistant to Wm. Madstard, was in 1641
chosen minister of the parish church of Kidderminster, and
exerted a wide and powerful influence upon the churches of
Worcestershire, and the religious controversies of England
throughout the Commonwealth, and after the Restoration,
till his death on Dec. 8, 1691 ; and, in his writings, onwards
to the present day.

After his settlement at Kidderminster in the place of
the incompetent vicar, Danse, Baxter had to withdraw
a while on account of the excitement of the rabble, who
cried, "Down with the Roundheads ; " and on his way
to Gloucester, as he passed but through a corner of the
suburbs of Worcester, they that knew him not cried,
"Down with the Roundheads," and he was glad to spur
on and be gone. "Coming to Gloucester," he continues,
" I found a civil, courteous, and religious people, as different
from Worcester as if they lived under a different Government. . . In Gloucestershire they were for the Parliament,

in Worcestershire wholly for the king. When I had been
at Gloucester a month, my neighbours of Kidderminster
came for me home. So I bid my host (Mr. Darney, the
town-clerk) and my friends farewell. After a time I was
fain to withdraw from Kidderminster again, and being with
one Mr. Hunt, near Inkborough, there came a party of the
Earl of Essex's army to block up Lord Byron in Worcester.
They lay in a meadow near Powick, above a mile from
Worcester, and I went to see them. There were several
excellent divines as chaplains to the several regiments, of
whom Mr. BIFIELD and Mr. MOOR quartered with us at
Kidderminster. The brigades in Kidderminster marched
off to Worcester, and seeing no safety in stopping at home,
and there was such excellent preaching among them at
Worcester, that I stayed there among them a few days.
Hereupon I was persuaded to go to Coventry, to stay with
Mr. Simon King, the minister, sometime schoolmaster with
me at Bridgenorth. After a month's stay, I complied with
a desire that I should preach to the soldiers once or twice a
week, and remained a year, following my studies as quietly
as in a time of peace." *

Baxter goes on to relate how he was induced to become
chaplain to Col. Whalley's regiment, which was sent to lay

---

* " During the siege (June, 1646) Dr. WARMESTRY and Richard Baxter took the oppor-
tunity of discoursing upon points of divinity. The first point which Baxter undertook to
defend was, that there was no difference between a church and any common place. They
disputed for several hours and parted friends." Nash, II., App. 98 ; *Reliquiæ Bax-
teriana*, 42-44.

siege to Worcester, and was there eleven weeks. "When
Worcester siege was over (having with joy seen Kidderminster and my friends there once again), the country being
now cleared, my old flock expected that I should return to
them."* In the course of another year Baxter returned
and prosecuted his pastoral work free from dispute and
religious strife, save a friendly controversy with Mr. JOHN
TOMBES, of Bewdley, a Worcestershire minister who held
Baptist views. JOHN TOMBES was born at Bewdley in 1602,
entered Magdalen Hall, Oxford, 1617, took his M.A., took
orders, and became Lecturer of St. Martin's, Carfax. In
1630 he became a preacher in Worcester, and thence
removed to Leominster. In 1653 he was appointed one of
the Triers for the County. He was a tower of strength
to the Baptists, and had many controversies. He afterwards
married and lived a retired life.†

Baxter had objected to enforce subscription to the
Solemn League and Covenant of 1643, and when, after the
execution of the king, the *Engagement* was issued for subscription by ministers and people in 1649, he used his
influence to prevent the Worcestershire ministers from
bringing it before their congregations ; except in Worcester
city, "where," he says, "I had no great interest and knew
not what they did." He had abundant encouragement in
the Lectures he preached at Worcester, Dudley, and other

* *Ibid.* p. 58.
† Wood's *Athenæ*, II., 556.

places. Some Episcopal ministers made no scruple of taking the *Engagement,* reading it :—"I will be true to the government of England [though at the present] without King or House of Lords" (p. 65). In 1652 Cromwell's forces passed through Kidderminster on their way to Worcester, where Charles II. was with the royalists, and kindly messages were sent to Baxter ; but, he writes, "I was at that time under so great an affliction of sore eyes, that I was scarce able to see the light, nor to stir out of doors" (p. 68). "After the battle, Kidderminster being but eleven miles from Worcester, the flying army passed through the town ; I was newly gone to bed when the noise of the flying horse acquainted us of the overthrow. The king went to Boscobell, where he was hid in an oak in a manner sufficiently declared to the world." *

Oliver's strength, adds Baxter, "lay in great part with the sectaries, *i.e.*, the Vanists, Seekers, Ranters and Quakers, whom the soldiers favoured, and I drew up a PETITION for the *ministry*, and got many thousand hands to it in Worcestershire. Regarding the sequestered clergy, six to one were by the oaths of witnesses proved to be insufficient, or scandalous, or both ; those who were able and godly ministers were cast out for war alone and as Royalists, and were comparatively few. Those put in were such as set themselves laboriously to seek the saving

* *Reliquiæ Baxterianæ,* p. 69.

of souls, though of necessity half of them were very young."*
Of his neighbour ministers, he says, "Our unity and concord was a great advantage. At Bewdley there was a church
of Anabaptists, at Worcester the Independents gathered
theirs ; but we were all of one mind and mouth and way."
His assistant in the ministry was RICHARD SERGEANT (p. 88),
and "when he was removed two miles from us, I got Mr.
HUMPHRY WALDERN to succeed him."

The Petition that Baxter refers to is entitled thus :—

"*The Humble Petition of many thousands, Gentlemen,
Freeholders, and others of the County of Worcester, to the
Parliament of the Commonwealth of England, in behalf of
the able, faithful, godly ministry of this nation.*" Delivered
by Col. JOHN BRIDGES and Mr. THOS. FOLEY, Dec. 22,
1652. Subscribed by above six thousand. With the
Parliament's answer thereto. The reply was as follows :—

> "The House commanded to give their thanks on the behalf
> of those of the County of Worcester that sent it, for their good
> affections expressed therein. And accordingly he did give them
> the thanks of the House, and that they would take their petition
> into serious consideration in due time."

> "It was the generality of the godly men who had been still
> for the Parliament that subscribed this petition ; it was not
> urged upon any, nor so much as sent to one half of the County

---

* P. 74. Further on, p. 82, he tells us, "Once riding on a great hot-mettled horse, as I
stood on a sidelong pavement in Worcester, the horse reared, and both his hinder feet slipt
from under him ; so that the full weight of the body of the horse fell upon my leg, which
yet was not broken, but only bruised."

or very near. And a great part of the County took only the hands of householders, and not sons, or servants, else many thousand more hands might quickly have been got." "I know," says Baxter, "none in England that have been closer tried whether they would raise a new war than the Worcestershire petitioners."

Over and above this Petition, Baxter (circ. 1652) drew up an AGREEMENT OF THE ASSOCIATED PASTORS AND CHURCHES OF WORCESTERSHIRE; the aim of his life being to unite Episcopalians, Presbyterians and Independents upon the main Gospel truths held in common by all, without compromise of their respective points of difference in non-essentials. Baxter opened his mind to his Brethren in a Meeting which he procured, after a Lecture, at WORCESTER. After several meetings, certain Heads of Agreement were unanimously adopted by the ministers of Worcestershire and some adjacent parts. The following is a List, published by a Quaker opponent in 1655,* of those who joined in the movement :—

RICHARD BAXTER, Teacher of the Church at Kiderminster.

JOHN BORASTON, Pastor of Kibsford and Bewdley.

RICHARD EADES, Pastor of Beckford, Gloucestershire.

CHARLES NOTT, Minister of Shelsey.

JAMES WARWICK, Minister at Hanley-Castle.

THOMAS EVANS, Minister at Welland.

---

* A true Testimony against the Pope's wayes. In a return to that Agreement of 42 of those that call themselves ministers of Christ (but are proved to be wrongers of men and of Christ) in the County of Worcester and some adjacent parts. Signed Richard Farnworth, the 8th day of the 11th month, 1655. March 20, 1655.

THO. WRIGHT, Teacher at Hartlebury.

*JOHN NOTT, Teacher at Sheriff Hales in Staffordshire.

*HENRY OSLAND, Teacher of the Church at Bewdley.

JOHN HILL, Minister at Clifton-upon-Thame.

*THO. BALDWINE, Minister at Wolverley.

*RICH. WOOLEY, Minister at Salwarpe.

JOHN FREESTON, Minister at Hampton Lovet.

*RICHARD SERGEANT (late of Stone), Preacher at Kiderminster.

*ANDREW TRUSTERAM, Pastor of the Church at Clent.

*THO. BROMWICH, Minister at Kemsey.

THO. FRANCKE, Teacher at Nanton-Beachamp.

JOHN TAYLER, Minister at Dudley.

*WILL. SPICER, Minister at Stone.

*HUMPHREY WOLDEN, Minister of Broome.

SAM. BOWATER, Rector of Astley.

*BENJAMIN BAXTER, Minister of Upton-upon-Severne.

WILL. LOLE, Minister at Priton.

THO. FRANCIS, Minister at Doderhill.

THO. JACKMAN, Minister at Barrough.

WILL. DURHAM, Pastor at Tredington.

THO. EASTON, Pastor at Batesford, Gloucestershire.

GILES COLLIER, Pastor of the Church at Blockley.

*GEORGE HOPKINS } Ministers at
THO. MATTHEWS } Evesham.

JOH. DALPHINE, Pastor of the Church at Honiborne.

JOSEPH TREBLE, Pastor of Church Lench.

WILL. WILLES, Preacher at Littleton.

RICH. BEESTON, Preacher at Breedon.

*WILL. KIMBERLEY, Preacher at Ridmerley.

*JOSEPH BAKER { Preachers in the
RICH. FINCHER { City of Worcester.

JO. WILLMOT, Preacher at Pershore.

FRA. HYATT, Minister at Eckington.

ROBERT BROWNE, Minister at White Lady Aston.

*GERVICE BRYAN, Pastor of the Church at Old Swineford and Sturbridge.

JOHN DEDICOTE, Preacher at Abbotesley.

The names marked with an asterisk are mentioned by Baxter himself in *Relig. Baxt.*, and he adds others who joined chiefly from other counties, viz. :—

Mr. WILSBY, of Womborne.

JOHN REIGNOLDS, of Wolverhampton.

JOSEPH ROCKE, of Rowley.

GILES WOOLEY.

AMBROSE SPARRY, of Martley.

Mr. DOWLEY, of Stoke.

JOHN SPILSBURY, of Bromsgrove.

Mr. JUICE, of Worcester.

EDWARD BOUCHIER, of Church-hill.

STEPHEN BAXTER.

"All of them worthy men, eminent for piety, moderation and ministerial abilities." Baxter also gives in full a statement dated Sept. 20, 1653, to this effect :—

> "We, whose names are under written, having had conference with divers of our brethren in the ministry of Worcestershire concerning their Agreement and Association . . do approve of their Christian intendments in the general.
>
> THO. WARMESTRY.
> THO. GOOD." *

In their ASSOCIATION the Ministers agreed upon a Monthly Meeting at certain market towns, and these were constantly kept up at Evesham and Kidderminster. They arranged to have lectures in every place in the county that had need. They chose four worthy men, Andrew Tristram, Henry Oasland, Thos. Baldwin, Jos. Treble, to preach one Sunday a month at places most in need. It was

---

* *Relig. Baxt.*, Part II., p. 149. "This is that Dr. Warmestry," adds Baxter, "who, when I was silenced by Bishop Morley, and he made Dean of Worcester, came purposely to my flock to preach those vehement tedious invectives, of which more hereafter."

called the Londoners' Lecture, because the Londoners gave pecuniary assistance in its support.

One of the Articles of Agreement ran thus :—

> XX. R. 1.—We judge it convenient to meet in five several Associations at five several places in the county, namely, at Worcester, Evesham, Upton, Kidderminster and Bromsgrove, and this once a month on a day to be agreed on (or oftener if need require).

> XX. R. 17.—We shall once a quarter, the 1st Friday of March, May, August and October (and oftener if urgent occasion require), send delegates from all these Associations, to Worcester, where we shall hold a more general meeting, for the resolving of greatest difficulties, and the more unanimous carrying on the work of the Gospel.

> 18.—We should admit into these our Associations the neighbour ministers also of other counties where no such Associations are, or are so remote that they can not well join in them.*

We meet with a "Judgment and Advice of the Associated Ministers of Worcestershire, held at Worcester, Aug. 6, 1658, concerning the endeavours of ecclesiastical peace and the Waies and Meanes of Christian Unity, which Mr. JOHN DUREV doth present; sent to him in the name and by the appointment of the aforesaid Assembly by Rich. Baxter, pastor of the church at Kidderminster, 1658." It contains the following brief but weighty statements :—

> "The Scripture is a Rule both plain and perfect, a heretic may misinterpret the words of any other Confession as well as

---

* *Christian Concord, or the Agreement of the Associated Pastors and Churches of Worcestershire; with Rich. Baxter's Explication and Defence of it,* 1653, pp. 14-17.

the words of Scripture. The remedie for Heresy is not to impose another Rule of faith than Scripture (as if this were insufficient and we could mend it). Subscribed in the name and by the appointment of the Assembly of the Associated Ministers of Worcestershire, held at Worcester, Aug. 6, 1658, by us :—

RICHARD BAXTER, pastor of the church at Kederminster.

JOHN BORASTON, pastor of the church at Bewdley.

THOMAS WRIGHT, pastor of the church at Hartlebury.

GILES COLLYER, pastor of the church at Blockley.

GEORGE HOPKINS, pastor of the church at Evesham.

JOSEPH TREBELL, pastor of the church at Church Lench."

It is noticeable that the signature of no minister resident in the city of Worcester appears to this letter, and that in the list of Associated Ministers the only names for Worcester itself are, JOSEPH BAKER and RICHARD FINCHER. In the *Parliamentary Survey of* 1650,* the following city ministers are mentioned : —

CITY OF WORCESTER. —St. Swithin's, ROWLAND CROSBY.

St. Clement's, noe minister.

St. Peter's [Cathedral] SIMON MOORE.

St. Hellen's and

St. Martin's, THOS. JUICE, by sequestration of former incumbent.

* Given in full at the end of this Volume in the Appendix.

St. Michael's in Bedwardine, SIMON MOORE.

All Saints', noe minister.

St. Nicholas, noe minister at present.

In the Lambeth Palace Library are many MS. volumes of *Augmentations of ministers' stipends,* and here in 1653 we find the following :—

All Saints' and Nicholas, in Worcester, RICHARD FINCHER, £50.

College, Peter's, Nicholas, and St. Michael's, SIMON MOORE, £50 (a godly painful minister).

Martin's, THO. JUICE, £20.

Relating specially to Simon Moore (or More) we have the following :—

" Whereas £300 a year was heretofore granted out of the Revenues of the Dean and Chapter of Worcester for mortgage of maintenance of the ministers of the city of Worcester, which was given 29 April 1649, settled on them by order of the Committee of the said County, as by order of the said Committee for Plundered Ministers 29 Nov. 1649 appeareth, by which Order the Trustees for the sale of Dean and Chapter lands were appointed to pay £150 for one half year's rent unto the said ministers ; And Mr. SIMON MORE and Mr. GILBERT COX, ministers of the said city, to whom there became due out of the said rents, June 24th last, one half year's rent, amounting to £150. It is ordered that Mr. Gervice Bucke, Receiver of

WORCESTER CATHEDRAL DURING THE COMMONWEALTH,

When the first Congregational Church in the City met for worship there.

the same, do forthwith pay unto the said ministers the said sum of £150, taking the said ministers their acquittances for the receipt thereof. Nov. 29, 1650." *

On the same topic the following occurs in the Edgar Tower MSS. in Worcester :—

"Order to John Tilte from the Committee for the city and county of Worcester for the payment of £20 out of the over-plus of moneyes remayning in his hands raised by the sale of lead for the repayring of the College Church at Worcester," to "Mr. SYMON MOORE, Minister of the Colledge att Worcester, being a very faithful preacher of God's Word, and of singular good affection to the Government of this Commonwealth," who had "suffered greate losses by the Scotch Army at Worcester." Signed by B. Lechmere and four others. 13 Sept. 1651.

"Order for a further sum of £10 to be paid to SIMON MOORE out of the overplus of money raysed of lead taken of the Colledge church to repaire and keep the same for *a publicke Meeting Place for the service of God.*" Jan. 17, 1652-3. †

" By the Committee for the City and County of Worcester.

Forasmuch as SIMON MOORE, minister of the Coll. of Worc. hath very small and incompetent maintenance for his great pains in preaching the Word and the performance of other ministerial offices there since his augmentation hath failed ; And for that there is some surplus of money yet remaining in Mr. John Tilt's hands of ye Money raised of lead taken off the College Church to repair and keep the same for a public Meeting Place

---

* Lambeth MSS. *Augmentations*, 979, fol. 455.

† *Hist. MSS. Commission, Fourteenth Report, Appendix Part VIII.*, pp. 188, 9.

for ye Service of God.   It is therefore thought fitt and ordered
that the said John Tilt shall pay unto Mr. SIMON MOORE Tenn
pounds out of the said surplus in his hands.   17 Jan. 1652.

GERVASE BUCKE.   WM. COLLINS.
JOHN NASH.   EDW. ELVINES.
THO. YOUNG.

Received from Mr. JOHN TYLT according to this present order,
the sum of ten pounds, Jan. 22, 1652,

By me, SIMON MOORE." *

From these documents it is clear that Symon Moore
was a distinguished man, and held a very important position
in the city of Worcester during the Commonwealth.   Baxter
calls him an old Independent ; the first Congregational
church formed in Worcester had him for its pastor, and the
Cathedral as its meeting-house.   The first notice we find of
Simon Moore is as a chaplain in the Parliament Army, when
he and another chaplain visited Baxter at Kidderminster.
Mr. Moore was chaplain to Lord Wharton's regiment, and,
says Baxter, "Mr. Bifield and Mr. Moor quartered with
us at Kiderminster."   Thence they soon marched off to
Worcester, and Baxter followed, "and there was such
excellent preaching among them at Worcester that I stayed
among them a few days.†   This was probably the occasion
of Moore's settlement in the city and at the Cathedral.
He is described as "a very faithful preacher of God's word,

---

* MS. in Edgar Tower, Bundle No. 9.   See also *Hist. MSS. Com. Report* 14, *Appendix
Part VIII.,* p. 188.

† *Reliquiæ Baxter.* pp. 42, 43.

and of singular good affection to the government of this Commonwealth,* who had suffered great losses by the Scotch army at Worcester." What the sufferings of the citizens were, is evident from the following :—

" To the Right Hon. the Counsell of State.

The humble petition of the Inhabitants of the Citty of Worcester sheweth : That the extreme poverty and sadd desolation of the citty of Worcester occasioned by the Scottish king coming thither in August last, and the unavoidable sacking of the said citty upon the reducing thereof and (since that) a great mortality amongst the principall inhabitants, hath putt an absolute incapacity upon that place to pay the arrears of contributions due from that citty, beeing a county of itselfe.

That a Troope of Coll. Tomlinson's regiment, now at Worcester demanding the Arreares of this last six months beeing £576 and take free quarter till it bee paid, which causeth the choice inhabitants and commoners to withdraw themselves and the remaining Commonalty almost to despair, they beeing soe farr from abilitie to pay that but for the charity of the out county of Worcester, who gave them £500, and the charity of some other places and persons, many families had certainly perished for want of bread.

* MS. in Edgar Tower ; *Hist. MSS Commission* 14th *Report, App. Part VIII.,* pp. 188, 9.

This being the true condition of that miserable place
your Petitioners humbly pray, that the said Troope may
bee ordered to some other place, and the arreares of contribution suspended, till the pleasure of the Parliament be
knowne, the peace as well as the necessity of that people
imploring it at your hands.   And they shall pray &c.

Signed in their name by me,

EDW. ELVINES." * [The Mayor].

Every effort was accordingly made in behalf of those
who thus suffered in the cause of liberty and of the Commonwealth.   Simon Moore, prominent as a sufferer was the
special object of the Counsell's care.   The proceeds of the
sale of lead from an old steeple belonging to the Cathedral
were devoted, first to the repair of the Almshouse and the
church itself, to be a Public Meeting Place for the Service
of God, and then to provide an adequate stipend for the
minister.

It is easy to explain the coolness that sprang up between
Simon Moore and Richard Baxter.   Moore believed in
Cromwell, Baxter did not.   Baxter regarded Oliver as a
self-seeking man, and did not shrink from plain censure of
him and his troops, in the pulpit.

> "The Committee men," he says, "looked sowre, but let me
> alone.   Yet none of the soldiers ever meddled with me, nor
> was I by any of them in those times forbidden or hindered to
> preach one sermon, except only one Assize sermon which the

* B. M. Add. MSS. 34, 326, fol. 54.

High Sheriff had desired me to preach, and afterwards sent me word to forbear, as from the Committee, saying that by Mr. MOOR's means (the Independent preacher at the Colledge), the Committee told him that they desired me to forbear, and not to preach before the Judges, because I preached against the State. But afterward they excused it as done merely in kindness to me, to keep me from running myself into danger and trouble." *

The following also relates to Simon Moore :—

"*Peter's in Worcester.* In pursuance of an order of the Trustees of Aug. 1, 1654. It is ordered that Captain John Silverwood, receiver, do from time to time pay unto Mr. SIMON MOORE, minister of Peter's, in the city of Worcester (approved according to the ordinance for approbation of publique preachers) the yearly summe of fowerscore and tenne poundes out of the rents and profitts of the impropriate tithes of Peter's in Worcester in possession of the said Trustees to be accounted from the 25th day of March 1655, and to be from time to time continued and paid unto him for such time as he shall discharge the duty of the minister of the said place, or until further order of the said Trustees. Provided that this order be first entered with the auditor. EDW. CRESSETT, RI. SYDENHAM, RA. HALL, JO. HUMFREY, JO. POCOCK. Dated Feb. 26, 1655." †

Worcester Cathedral Officers.—" Upon the humble petition of John Sayers, Richard Browne, John Biddle, Nicholas Cottrell, and John Leight, officers of the late Cathedral of Worcester, it is ordered that the summe of £20 be paid unto them out of the arreares of rent due before Jan. 6, 1649,

* *Reliquiæ Baxterianæ*, Part I., p. 67.
† Lambeth MSS. *Augmentations*, 972, fol. 419.

towards their releife, to be distributed by Mr. Hopkins.
And Mr. Lawrence Steele, Treas., is to pay the same
accordingly (fol. 103, 106). To the poore officers of the
Cathedral of Worcester £20 to be distributed unto them by
Mr. Hopkins according to their respective necessities.
Dated Nov. 22, 1655." *

Provision was also made for the other ministers of the
city :—

Dec. 10, 1656.

"*Andrew's in Worcester.* In pursuance of an order of his
Highness and the Councell of July 10, 1656. It is ordered that
the yearly summe of £50 be and the same is hereby granted
to the Minister of Andrew's in the city of Worcester, to and
for increase of his maintenance. And it is further ordered
that the said £50 a year be from time to time payd unto
Mr. JOSEPH BAKER, Minister of Andrew's in Worcester aforesaid (approved according to the ordinance for approbation
of publique preachers, Nov. 16, 1656), out of the rents and
profitts hereafter mentioned.†

April 28, 1657.

Upon consideration had of the Petition of the Parishioners of
Andrew's and *Hellen's* in Worcester, prayeing the discharging
of the arreares of tenths due out of the said parishes to these
Trustees, as also the payment of the Augmentation of £50 a
year to Mr. BAKER minister there, from the time of his settlement ; It is ordered that Captain John Silverwood, Receiver,
do certifie unto these Trustees how long the said tenths have

* Lambeth MSS. *Augmentations*, 967, fols. 96, 103, 106.
† Lambeth MSS. *Augmentations*, 972, fol. 633.

been in arreare, and how much they amount unto; where-upon they will take the said petition into further consideration.*

Similar grants were voted by the Council of State in London during the Protectorate to RICHARD FINCHER of All Saints and Nicholas, £50, THOS. JUICE, of Martin's, £20.†

Provision was also made during the Protectorate for a Schoolmaster of the Free School :—

Nov. 22, 1655.

Worcester Schoole. Whereas the yearly stipend of £15 heretofore payable by the Dean and Chapter of Worcester to the Schoolmaster of the FREE SCHOOL of Worcester, together with a diett allowance in the Colledg of Worcester, in lieu whereof he hath received £5 a yeare ; And whereas there hath been a further yearly allowance due unto the said schoolmaster from the said Dean and Chapter in wheate and barley amount-ing to £10 a year ; which said several sums amount in all unto £30 a year. It is therefore ordered, that the said yearly summe of £30 be from time to time paid unto Mr. THOMAS BAREFOOTE, schoolmaster of ye said schoole, out of the rents and profitts of the tithe-corne of Clewe Pryor, in the Co. of Wor-cester, from March 25 last, and to be continued and paid to Mr. BAREFOOTE, for such time as he shall discharge the duty of schoolmaster there.‡

The following is interesting concerning the *Pentecostals* or Whitsun-farthings, a sum raised at a farthing per head from the householders in a chapelry or dependent church,

* Lambeth MSS. *Augmentations*, 974, fol. 405.
† Lambeth MSS. *Aug.* 972, fols. 76, 168, 296 ; *Aug.* 981, fol. 141.
‡ Lambeth MSS. *Augmentations*, 967, fol. 13.

and paid to the mother church at Whitsuntide. They are
mentioned in a grant of Henry VIII. to the Dean and
Chapter of Worcester. They amounted for Worcester to
about £5.*

June 26, 1656.

Mr. Richardson, Dean and Chapter of Worcester, Whitsun
Farthings.—It is ordered that Stephen Richardson of the City
of W., gent., doe and he is hereby authorised and appointed
from time to time to collect gather and receive all oblations
commonly called by the name of Whitson Farthings payable to
the Dean and Chapter of W. and arising and becoming due
and payable out of several parishes in the Counties of Worcester, Hereford, and elsewhere, and all arreares thereof.
And all person and persons by whom the same are payable
are hereby appointed and required to pay the same unto him
the said Mr. Stephen Richardson ; and it is further ordered
that all such persons as shall refuse to pay unto the said
Stephen the arreares of the said Whitsun Farthings from them
respectively due, doe by themselves or by some other person
or persons by them sufficiently authorised in that behalf,
answer their neglect before these Trustees on the 4th Nov. next.
JO. THOROWGOOD, ED. CRESSETT, JO. HUMFREY, JO. POCOCK,
RICH. YOUNG.†

* Noake's *Notes and Queries*, 23, 56.
† Lambeth MSS. *Augmentations*, 974, fols. 165, 322.

V.

The Nonconformist Persecution.

ISERABLE as was the Stuart Dynasty in its four successive kings, it accomplished one good thing; it brought out the noblest heroism of the English race both in Church and State. The goodly company of Puritan Refugees; the Pilgrim Fathers, founders of the United States; Milton, Oliver Cromwell, and the statesmen of the noble army of the Commonwealth; Nonconformists driven from their cures; these we owe to the contemptible pedantry of James, to the untrustworthy lawlessness of Charles I., to the dissolute meanness of Charles II., and to the Romish deceptions of the second James. Perhaps the highest act of heroism was under the notorious ACT OF UNIFORMITY, when nearly three thousand God-fearing ministers were driven from their cures, into silence and poverty, fine and imprisonment. They might have remained; a stroke of the pen, a single signature was all required. But rather than sign they

would have cut off their right hand, rather than violate
conscience they would have gone to the scaffold.   That
treacherous and deceitful Act, violating the pledges given
upon the Restoration, swept the learned, true, and good
from the churches, and brought in in shoals the incompetent,
the cruel, the unscrupulous. Worcestershire, like every other
English county, is full of illustrations of this.   Take one
example.   At Kidderminster laboured the holy, loveable
RICHARD BAXTER, author of *The Saint's Rest*.   He had
come thither twenty years before, at the unanimous call of
the parishioners, who had as unanimously petitioned for
the removal of the former incumbent (one Dance) as
"utterly insufficient for the ministry, presented by a Papist,
unlearned, preached but once a quarter, and then in such a
way as to expose him to laughter, and a frequenter of Ale-
houses."   This man knowing his unfitness compounded
the business, keeping his income of £200 a year, and paying £60 for Baxter to do the work.   For twenty years, in
season, and out of season, Baxter laboured in the pulpit,
and from house to house, producing a revival and reformation that is traceable even still.   To George Morley, the
Restoration Bishop of Worcester, is due the crime of silenc-
ing Richard Baxter, and like a wolf among the sheep, of
making havoc of his church, imprisoning the most pious and
upright among them.   Baxter might have been a bishop ;
he was offered the bishopric of Hereford ; but on conditions
which meant the violation of truth and conscience, of those

very Protestant principles, which Morley had before himself professed. Morley sits in his episcopal throne, Dance is restored at Kidderminster, and Baxter is driven as a fugitive through the land, in poverty, and in prisons oft.

Calumny was the usual clerical weapon against the Nonconformists of that day ; and it is a weapon wielded still, though happily our civil and religious liberties, so dearly won, secure us against fine and imprisonment. The *Christian Knowledge Society* is publishing a series of popular little volumes, entitled, *Diocesan Histories*, and in the *Worcester* volume we find the following statement regarding Richard Baxter :—

> "When Baxter wished to take the place of Mr. Dance as Vicar of Kidderminster, he wrote freely of him, not only as a week and ignorant man who preached only once a quarter, but as 'a frequenter of ale houses, and sometimes drunk.' But when afterwards confronted with Bishop Morley, and aware that he would have to give proof of his assertions, his tone was altered. According to the bishop's account, which seems to be uncontradicted, he said then of Dance that he was a man of unblameable life and conversation, though not of such parts as would fit him for the care of so great a congregation." *

---

* *Diocesan Histories, Worcester,* by J. Gregory Smith and Phipps Onslow, 1893, p. 233. Besides the *blots* above quoted, the book contains many errors. Juice, of St. Martin's is named "*Juse*" (p. 248) ; the Parliamentary Survey of 1650 is styled "an Inquisition of 1653" (p. 250). On p. 252 it is affirmed that "Baxter never administered the Lord's Supper," whereas Baxter speaks of having 600 communicants, *Reliquiæ Baxterianæ,* part I. p. 85. SIMON MOORE, the Independent minister of the Cathedral is in one place designated "*Richard* Moore" (p. 243), and on another page we are told he "had taken possession of the Cathedral," (p. 260), the truth being that he had been appointed minister there by the then existing authorities.

This statement is false and calumnious from beginning to end. Any honest man who knows Baxter's life and writings would at once repudiate it. Baxter did not endeavour to supplant Dance ; he did not accuse Dance ; the accusations were made to the Parliament Committee by Dance's own parishioners, who having come to an arrangement with Dance, invited Baxter (as we have narrated) to preach at Kidderminster, and then unanimously elected him. Dance was afterwards sequestered by the Parliament, but Baxter never removed him from the Vicarage house ; " so far was I," writes Baxter, " from seizing it as my own, or removing him out of the town. But he lived in peace and quietness with us, and reformed his life." * This gives the lie to the slander that Baxter, before Bishop Morley, "changed his tone when aware that he would have to give proof of his assertions." " I was somewhat wearied," writes Baxter, " to be every day caluminated and hear new slanders raised of me." As to Bishop Morley's account being " uncontradicted," though Baxter, like Christ before Pilate, bore the accusations silently, more than one reply was published in vindication of Baxter. The writers of this new calumny need to be reminded of the Ninth Commandment. It is a pity that a respectable and useful society should unwittingly be made the vehicle of it.

In the city of Worcester four able and godly men—all Independents and Pastors of Congregational churches,

* *Relig. Baxter.*, Part I. page 97.

KING EDGAR'S TOWER, A.D. 1005.

Where the Old Records of the See, the Bishops' Registers,
and the *Acta*, &c. are kept.

were driven from their cures. *First* was SIMON MOORE,
"the old Independent," as Baxter styles him, whose congregation was gathered in the Cathedral. He had as his
assistant for a time, Mr. Gilbert Cox. In his place came
the new bishop, Morley, of whom we have spoken, with a
long train of ecclesiastics, dean and canons, exchanging the
simplicity of Congregationalism for prayer-book Royalism
in ritual and dogma. Simon Moore was through the fury
and rage of the consistory and the mob, harrassed, fined,
robbed, and imprisoned, and at length compelled to leave
Worcester. In the *Acta* of the Bishop's court, we find
among hosts of names of honest and pious citizens who
would worship God according to their conscience, the
following :—

"Feb. 1664. *St. Peter's*, Worcester. *Contra Magis-
trum* SIMONEM MORE, *presentat.* for not coming to his
parish church." *

Usually this charge was followed up by fine, excommunication, and imprisonment. At the sacrifice of home,
and property, and friends, the good man was at length
compelled to leave the city. He went to London, and his
name occurs among the eminent ministers who found their
refuge in the great city, and preached as occasion served. †

Secondly, we have THOMAS JUICE, son-in-law to Simon
Moore, and also an Independent Minister, gathering his

---

* *Acta* of the Consistory Court, kept in the Edgar Tower.
† Calamy, *Account*, p. 53, 768, 9 ; *Contin.* 77, 884.

church in *St. Martin's.* He was "a sober, grave, serious, peaceable, blameless, able minister. He lost £100 *per annum* by his ejection. And afterwards for a livelihood for himself, his wife, and three children, he taught a little school, till the Corporation Act took place, when he was forced to abscond. He was afterwards pastor of a congregation at Reading, in Berkshire, and there died before the end of the century."[*]

Thirdly. From *All Saints'* and *Nicholas* was ejected Mr. RICHARD FINCHER, a moderate Independent, a zealous, able preacher, and of a good life.[†] At first he taught a school for his support, and in 1669 took part in preaching at the house of Mr. Thomas Stirrup and Mr. Thos. Smyth every second Sunday.[‡] He took out a licence to preach upon Charles II.'s *Indulgence* of 1672. "Licence to Richard Fincher to be a Congregational Teacher in the house of Richard Cornton, in Worcester."[§] He afterwards became pastor of the church in Unicorn Yard, London. He died Feb. 10, 1692-3, and his funeral sermon was preached by the excellent Mr. Slater, and afterwards published. Mr. Slater writes:—

> "In all my conversation with RICHARD FINCHER I found him to be of a sweet, affable, loving temper. He had good natural parts, which were cultivated and improved by acquired learning.

[*] Calamy, *Account*, p. 769.
[†] *Reliquiæ Baxterianæ*, Part III., 91.
[‡] Lambeth MSS., 639, fol. 272.
[§] R.O. Preachers' Licences, Charles II., 1671-2.

He had found mercy to be faithful, having been so all along to his great Lord and Master, standing his ground like a rock unshaken in the days of sorest and most violent temptation. Yet he was a man of peace, and would follow it with all men, so far as he could go without forsaking truth and holiness. He was a very modest person, clothed with humility. He was a workman that needed not to be ashamed. He died Feb. 10, 1692-3." [*]

Fourth. From *St. Andrews* went forth JOSEPH BAKER, a learned man, of a blameless life ; one who preached constantly, and catechised the people, and conferred with the several families (especially before he first admitted them to the Lord's Supper) personally. He was a man of extraordinary prudence, calmness, patience, gravity, and soundness of judgment. Neither for prelacy, presbytery, nor Independency, as then formed into parties ; but for that which was found in all the parties, and for concord upon such catholic terms. The parish of St. Andrew, where he was minister, had but about £6 a year maintenance, of which he took none, but gave it to a woman to teach the poor children of the parish to read, living upon his own, and some small Augmentation granted by the Parliament.[†]

Mr. Joseph Read asked him upon his death bed what thoughts he then had of his Nonconformity. He answered that "he gladly would have continued the exercise of his Ministry, if he could have had liberty for it, without sin

[*] Wilson's *Diss. Churches,* IV. 228-230.
[†] *Reliquiæ Baxterianæ,* Part III., pp. 90, 91.

against God ; but when it came to that, there was no remedy." * He removed to Old Swinford, where Thomas Foley lived ; and here he died ; and a monument in the chancel of the church bears this inscription :—

"*Reverendus Josephus Baker obiit* 25 *Mar.* A.D. 1668, *æt.* 42.

Juxta S.E. supradicti Josephi frater germanus Johannes, natus 1631, *denatus Dec.* 6, 1678." †

Thus it is clear that Congregationalism in Worcester had its origin in the Cathedral itself, St. Peter's and St. Michael's, when the first Independent church was gathered, and so widely spread among the citizens that other congregations were gathered after the same order in St. Martin's, All Saints' and Nicholas, and St. Andrew's, under the pastorate of three other Independent ministers. Though scattered by the penal laws of the Restoration these churches still worshipped in secret conventicles amid the storm of hate and persecution till the Indulgence of 1672, and of 1687 followed by the Toleration Act, enabled them to build their own places of worship and bear public witness to the truths of New Testament Christianity.

Fifth. We now come to the name of a fifth nonconforming minister, himself a native of Worcester, who began to exercise his ministry immediately after the passing of

* Calamy, *Account*, 1. 769.
† Nash, II. 215.

the Act of Uniformity, in 1663. He gathered round him as their pastor the scattered members of those Independent churches that had worshipped in the Cathedral and other parishes of Worcester during the Commonwealth, and who as sheep without a shepherd were harassed, fined and imprisoned, because they would not attend the new establishment, nor partake of the sacrament kneeling in the Romanist manner. His name was THOMAS BADLAND. The family was one of high standing in the county. Richard Badland, an ancestor, perhaps grandfather, was Bailiff of the city of Worcester in 1566,* and the name of John Badland occurs in the charter of the city given by James I., Oct. 2, 1621.† Thomas Badland was born in Worcester in the year 1634. He became minister of Willenhall, Staffordshire, in 1656. We find his name among the ministers who gave certificates to John Oxford as minister of Arley, in Staffordshire, in 1658 (Nov. 10). The names are, "Henry Osland, Ri. Fincher, THO. BADLAND OF WILLENSHALL, John Wheeler, Fr. Bromwich, John Women, John Tayler."‡ Thus he appears side by side with Richard Fincher and other well known Worcestershire ministers in recommending John Oxford. From Willenhall Thomas Badland was ejected for Nonconformity in 1662, and he came at once to Worcester, his native city, where he had relations, and where he found a ministerial

* Nash, *App.* 112.

† Valentine Green, *Hist. of W.,* I. 36.

‡ Lambeth MSS. *Augmentations* 999, No. 415. Oxford married Elizabeth Foley of Old Swinford.

F

friend and brother in Richard Fincher. He then was a young man of 29 years, but he at once began to gather the Nonconformists to worship at the risk of fine and imprisonment. The *Acta* of the Bishop's court (now in the Edgar tower) are full of names of citizens cited, fined, excommunicated, and imprisoned; their only crime being non-attendance at church, or at the Communion. The following may serve as examples :—

"*St. Clement's.* Ri. Chandler presented for not coming to church, and not receiving the sacrament at times appointed. James Chandler, James and Mary Russell, ditto.

St. Martin's. Arthur Jones, for not baptizing his child. John Dawby, Wm. Hughes, for not coming.

St. Peter's. Valentine Combe, for working upon holy days, especially upon Candlemas day last past. Constantine Moule.

St. Nicholas. Thos. Ince, for keeping school without licence, and not coming to the sacrament. John Carpenter, Fran. Haynes, ditto.

St. Andrew's in Worc. John Watts, Thos. Haywood, John Timbs, John Tyler, R. Woodward, John Roberts, for not coming to church to hear divine service upon Sundays and holy days.

St. Clement's. James Elley.

      Contr. Henry Baldwin, senior, for not constantly frequenting his parish church, neither receiving the sacrament.

      William Adney, for not receiving the Sacrament at Easter last and other times.

      John Dawson, Jacob King, John Davies,

Edm. Pritchett and his wife.

Mary, wife of Thos. Price, for not coming to her parish church.

St. Helen's in Worc.   John Wolley,* schoolmaster, for working upon holy days, especially upon St. Andrew's day, Nov. 7, 1664.

Michael Hacket and Roger Clark [Mayor in 1685], for not coming, &c.

St. Swithen's.   John Bearcroft [Mayor in 1669], Wm. Swift.†

St. Michael's.   Peter Rogers, John Cowles, ditto.

All Saint's.   Ambrose Meredith, Wm. Wheeler.

St. Peter's.   Mr. SIMON MOOR, for not coming to his parish church, Ri. Yarnold, Wm. Elley, Thos. Cooke, Walter Bradley." ‡

The usual course was first, presentation and admonition ; then fine ; next excommunication and imprisonment. Calamy mentions two or three cases.   Mr. Ri. Wooley, ejected from Salwarpe, who came to live in Worcester, was indicted "for not coming to church, and for keeping meetings.   A warrant was issued to levy £20 upon him. All his cattle to the value of £40 were hereupon driven away from him, and bought by the wayside for £15 by a friend of Mr. Wooley's, and at that rate he had them again. The constable was afterwards forced to levy £5 more upon his goods, which he also paid.   Another person was forced to pay £10, and £10 more was levied upon several other

* Ejected minister of Broomsgrove, Nash, I. 167.

† Buried in St. Swithen's, where is a family monument.   " In memory of William Swift of this city, Esq., who was buried Feb. 20, 1688." Nash, II., App. 119.

‡ *Acta* in Cupboard, Edgar Tower, 1664.

hearers, some of them being day labourers, which lay very heavy.   One Mr. ROBERT HUMPHREYS, an Anabaptist preacher and inhabitant of the parish of Claines, two miles from Worcester, for preaching in his house, had by a warrant three cows taken from him, worth about £15, and all the goods in his house that were of any value ; and he could never get anything restored.   And one Mr. WM. PARDOE, of the same persuasion, who lived at Tenbury, for not going to his parish church was excommunicated, and by a writ *de excom. cap.* was committed to the county goal, where he remained about six years to April 1671.   God grant we may never see such doings more." *

To understand these proceedings it must be remembered that the *Act of Uniformity* in 1662 was followed by the *Conventicle Act,* July 1, 1664, "for suppressing seditious Conventicles, inflicting on all persons above the age of sixteen, present at any religious meeting in other manner than is allowed by the Church of England, where five or more persons beside the household should be present, a penalty of three months' imprisonment for the first offence, of six for the second, and of seven years' transportation for the third, on conviction before a single justice of peace." Again, the Oxford or *Five Mile Act,* Oct. 31, 1665, enacted that those who refused the oath, "I will not at any time endeavour any alteration of government in Church or State," shall be incapable of teaching in any public or

* Calamy's *Account*, I. p. 776.

private schools, or of taking any boarders, under pain of
£40; and shall not come or be within five miles of any
city, town-corporate or borough, or within five miles of any
parish, town or place wherein they have been parson."

As the people for the most part refrained from accusations under these persecuting Acts, the Bishops sent letters
of enquiry to all the clergy, making them informers against
the Nonconformists. The following is the letter of the
Bishop of Worcester, Walter Blandford :—

The Bp. to the Clergy of the Places where Conventicles were kept.

SIR, having received an order dated June 8, 1669, requiring
me by the assistance of Parish Ministers and others to make
strict and diligent enquiry within my diocese as well as in
places peculiar and exempt as those of my own proper
jurisdiction :—

1. What and how many conventicles or unlawful assemblies
under pretence of religion are held in every town and parish,
and in whose houses?

2. What are the number that usually meet at them, and how
often?

3. Of what sect, condition, and sort of people they consist?

4. Who are their ministers and teachers, the leading or
principal persons frequenting and promoting their meetings?

5. What authority they pretend and from whom, and from
what ground they look for impunity?

I do hereby require you by virtue of the said order, that
some time before the 14th of the next month, you deliver or
cause to be delivered to me in writing under your hand (according to the several articles of enquiry above mentioned) a true

and particular account of such unlawful proceedings under
pretence of religion as are or lately have been within your
parish, that so I may give notice (as you also are from time to
time to do) to the Justices of the Peace for the suppressing of
them.   Yours affec.   W. W.*

We have not succeeded in finding the replies sent by
the Worcestershire clergy, but in Lambeth the Returns
are imperfectly given for the various Dioceses (*see* Appendix)
and here is that for the city of Worcester, 1669 :—

Parish.	*Sects.*	*Numbers.*	*Quality.*	*Heads and Teachers.*
St. Nicholas in Worc. Att the houses of Mr. THOS. STIRRUP and Mr. THOS. SMYTH, every second Sunday.		About 200.	Of all sorts. Some people of good sufficiency.	Mr. RICHARD FINCHER, Mr. THOMAS BADLAM (*sic*) Nonformists.
Another in the house of Mr. JOHN EDWARDS in the parish aforesaid.		About 40.	Of all sorts, and of good accompt.	Unknowne.†

Within three years after this, Charles II. stayed this
Prelatical espionage and persecution by issuing his DECLARA-
TION OF INDULGENCE, March 15, 1671–2. It declares "that
the execution of all penal laws against Nonconformists be
immediately suspended, and this our Indulgence as to the
allowance of public places of worship, and approbation of
the preachers shall extend to all sorts of Nonconformists."

---

* In a file of letters deposited by the late Bishop of Worcester in the Edgar Tower.
† Lambeth MSS. 639, fol. 272.

Under this, the following places and persons were licensed in the City of Worcester.

177   Licence to Thomas Badland to be a Pr. Teacher in the house of Wm. Cheatle, in Worcester. 22 April, 1672.

      The house of Wm. Cheatle, in Worcester, licenced for a Pr. Meeting Place. 22 Apr., 1672.

      Licence to Rich. Fincher to be a Congregational Teacher in the house of Rich. Cornton, in Worcester.

      The house of Rich. Cornton, in Worcester, licenced for a Pr. Meeting Place.

      The house of Eliz. Stirrup, in Worcester, licenced for a Pr. Meeting Place, 22 July, 1672.

      Licence to Rich. Wooley to be a Pr. Teacher in the house of Eliz. Stirrup, in Worcester. 22 July, 1672.

251   Licence to Rich. Wooley to be a Pr. Teacher at his own house, in the city of Worcester. Sept. 20, 1672.

257   The house of Rich. Wooley, in the city of Worcester, Pr. Sept. 30, 1672.

273   The house of Rich. Smith, of ye city of Worcester, Pr. Nov. 18, 1672.

      The house of Ann Sworle, of the citty of Worcester, Pr. Dec. 9, 1672.*

Thus it appears that three nonconforming ministers, Thos. Badland, Rich. Fincher and Rich. Wooley ejected from Salwarpe, who had come to live in Worcester, took out Licences to preach under the conditions of the *Indulgence* of 1671-2, and that six places for religious worship,

* Record Office, S. P. *Dom.* Ch. II., Preaching Licences, 380.

Presbyterian or Independent, were licenced, namely the dwelling-houses of Wm. Cheatle, Rich. Cornton, Elizabeth Stirrup, Richard Wooley, Richard Smith and Ann Sworle.

The respite and calm produced among the harrassed Nonconformists did not last above two years. In the course of the next year the king cancelled it, and the fear of Popish ascendancy prompted Parliament to pass the *Test Act*, March 25, 1673-4, which rendered the reception of the sacrament according to the Establishment, and a renouncing of the dogma of transubstantiation, a necessary condition for government appointments. The high church or court party preached passive obedience, and enforced these laws against Nonconformists. Thus persecution with Judge Jeffries as its minister, and the clergy as its abettors, continued till the death of the king. During the first year of James II.'s reign some of the Episcopal clergy continued their obsequious betrayal of the liberties of their countrymen, but the latitudinarian party awoke the hostility of the king, who was a Romanist, and who, for the sake of Romanists, relaxed the penal statutes and issued, April 4, 1687, a *Declaration for Liberty of Conscience*, suspending all penal laws against Nonconformity, and abrogating all acts which imposed a religious test. The Nonconformists generally, while they took advantage of their new liberty, joined hands with their fellow Protestants within the Establishment against the common danger now threatening the country, and rejoiced in the acquittal of the seven bishops who refused to recognize the king's dispensing power.

This was the year, 1687, when the Nonconformists of Worcester adopted, as pastor and people united, *their Christian profession and covenant.* The news of the landing of the Prince of Orange was hailed with joy by them, and in the first year of William and Mary the *Toleration Act* was passed.

VI.

The Pastors of the Angel Street Congregational Church.

1.—The Rev. Thomas Badland.

1663-1698.

ORE suffering for conscience sake during five and twenty years had not crushed, it had strengthened the fortitude and faith of the Worcester Nonconformists; and now that liberty of worship dawns for them, the page of history records their *Christian Profession and Covenant,* couched in clear and solemn words, and signed by a goodly band of faithful followers of Christ, united in fellowship to HIM as their Divine Head, and under the care of the wise and brave pastor who had ministered to them all through those years of persecution. We rank Thomas Badland first of the Angel Street Pastors, and give in full and in *facsimile* the Document we have named.

" 1687.—The record of a particular Church of Christ at Worcester, consisting of Pastor and people united in the Christian profession and covenant following.

We do beleive that there is one only God ; the Father, Infinite in being, wisdom, goodnesse and power ; the maker, preserver and disposer of all things, and the most just and mercifull Lord of all. Wee beleive that mankind being fallen by sin from God and happinesse, under the wrath of God, the curse of his law, and the power of the devill : God so loved the world that he gave his only Son to be their Redeemer : who being God, and one with the Father, did take to him our nature, and became man, being conceived of the Holy Ghost in the Virgin Mary, and borne of her, and named Jesus Christ : and having lived on earth without sin, and wrought many miracles for a witnesse of his truth, he gave up himselfe a sacrifice for our sins, and a ransome for us, in suffering death on the crosse : And being buried, he rose againe the third day, and afterward ascended into heaven, where he is Lord of all in glory with the Father : And having ordained that all that truly repent and beleive in him, and love him above all things, and sincerely obey him, and that to the death, shall be saved ; and they that will not shall be damned ; and commanded his ministers to preach the gospell to the world. He will come againe, and raise the bodies of all men from the dead, and will set all the world before him to be judged according to what they have done in the body. And he will

adjudge the righteous to life everlasting, and the rest to everlasting punishment, which shall be executed accordingly.

We beleive that God the Holy Ghost, the Spirit of the
Father and the Son was sent from the Father by the Son,
to inspire and guide the prophets and Apostles that they
might fully reveal the doctrine of Christ.   And by multitude of evident miracles and wonderfull gifts to be the
great witnesse of Christ, and of the truth of his holy Word :
and to dwell and work in all that are drawen to beleive,
that being first joyned to Christ their head, and into one
Church which is his body, and so pardoned, and made the
Sons of God, they may be a peculiar people sanctified to
Christ : And may mortify the flesh, and overcome the
world and the Devill ; and being zealous of good works,
may serve God in holinesse and righteousnesse : And may
live in the speciall love and communion of the saints, and
in hope of Christ's coming and of everlasting life.

We do heartily take this one God for our only God and our
cheif good, and this Jesus Christ for our only Lord, Redeemer
and Saviour, and this Holy Ghost for our Sanctifier ; and
the doctrine by Him revealed and sealed by His miracles,
and now contained in the Holy Scriptures we do take for
the law of God and the rule of our fayth and life.   And repenting unfeignedly of our sins, we do resolve through the Grace
of God sincerely to obey Him, both in holinesse to God and
righteousnesse to men, and in speciall love to the Saints,
and communion with them, against all the temptations of

the Devill, the world, and our owne flesh, and this to
the death.

THOMAS BADLAND Pastour.

William Hodges.

Mr. Ths. Wooley.

Mr. Allex. Bearcroft.

Mr. Wildy.

Elizab. Badland.

Mrs. Hannah Stirrup.

Mrs. Mary Cook.

Mrs. Eliz. Stirrup.

Margaret Lokier.

Jane Hanking.

Eliza Brown.

Mr. Joseph Richards
and his wife Elenor.

Henry Neale

Rich. Wheeler
and An his wife.

Eliz. Walker.

Katherine Blackwell.

Mr. Wm. Chetle.

Mr. Thos. Smith.

Mr. John Beard
and his Wife.

Mrs. Sarah Chetle.

Mrs. Elizab. Chetle.

Mrs. Dorothy Woolly.

Mrs. Mary Longmore.

Mrs. Eliz. Dolman.

Mrs. Abigall Higgins.

Margaret Tayler.

Ann Owen.

Cisely Fincher.

Elizabeth Luggon.

Margaret Wells.

Joseph Fincher.

Bridget Smith.

Miss Mary Walton.

John Kent.

Mrs. Sarah Chetle,
daught. to Mr. William Chetle.

Mrs. Anne Harris,
wife to Mr. Ric. Harris.

Mr. John Evans
and his wife Anne."

all yt are drawen to believe, yt 3
being first joyned to Christ their
head, and into one Church wch
is his body, and so pardoned, and
made ye sons of god, they may be
a peculiar people sanctified to Christ
And may mortify yr flesh, and
overcome ye world & ye devill:
And being zealous of good works,
may serve god in holinesse and
righteousnesse, And may live in
ye spiriall love and comunion of
ye saints, and in hope of Christs
comming, and of overlasting life.

We do heartily take this one god for
or only god, and or cheif good, and
his Jesus Christ for or only lord,
redeemer and saviour, and this
holyghost for or sanctifier; and
ye doctrine by him revealed
and sealed by his miracles, and
now contained in ye holy scriptures
we do take for ye law of god,
and ye rule of or fayth and life.
And repenting unfaignedly of or
sins we do resolve through ye
grace of god sincerely to obey him
both in holinesse to god and
righteousnesse to men, and

4] in speciall *comunion* of the saints, and
comunion with them, against all
the temptations of the Devill, the world
and of owne flesh, and this
to the death.

Thomas Badland Pastour

William Hodgtt   mr Wm Chitle
mr Jho Woolly
mr Alles *vincials*   mr Jho Smith.
mr o Wildy
Elizal Badland   mr John Bound
mr Hannah *Shirrow*   & his wife
mr o Mary Cook   mr o Sarah Cokes
mr o Eliz. *Shirrow*   mr o Elizal Chitle
Margtry *Lubiet*   mr o Dorothy Woolly
Jane Hankins   mr o Mary Longmor
Eliza Brown.   mr o Elid. Holman
mr Jhon Rikords   mr o Abigal Higgins
& his w. Elinor   Margery Taylor
Henery Nailer   Ann Owen
Rich. Nailer   Cisley finder
& An his wife   Elizuk Suggon
Eliz Wilker   Margery Wolls
Katherin Blackwel   Joseph *Ainslos*

Mrs Sarah Chotle
daught to Mr
William Chitce
Bridget Smith
Mr & mary Walton
John. Kent.
Mr Anne Harris.
wife to mr Rr. Harris
Mr John Evans.
& & wife Ann

"The number of communicants," says Mr. Samuel Blackwell in his MS., "added in Mr. Badland's hand-writing is forty. After 1687 to Feb. 22, 1699, it is 120. The place of worship was at the lower end of Fish Street where the front part of the Porcelain Manufactory now stands [now Dent's glove manufactory], but no part of the old building now remains. It had been lighted up at night by three small brass Chandeliers which, with some iron candlesticks to stick into pillars, and some of the wainscot of the pews, were made use of in the present Meeting-house."

"The usual religious services were on Lord's Day morning and afternoon; occasionally in the evening. The clerk began with singing. Then a short introductory prayer. Then a portion of the Old, and a portion of the New Testament. Then a hymn; and a long prayer before sermon. After sermon a Psalm or hymn, a short prayer, and the usual blessing concluded. The Lord's Supper was administered every two months; and there was a preparatory service on the Thursday preceding. When any person wished for communion, the Minister, after satisfactory private interview, stated to the Communicants at the conclusion of the next ordinance, that A, B, or C, (naming them) desired Communion at the next Sacramental service. No allowable objection having been made, the Minister announced to the assembled Communicants that A, B, or C, having been proposed at the last service were there and then to take their places. The collection for the poor was made from pew to pew by the Elders while the last hymn was being sung."

Among the places of religious worship certified under the Toleration Act for Protestant Dissenters is the following:—

"Worcester, Warmstree House, certified for religious worship of Protestant Dissenters by THOMAS BADLAND, 1 October, 1689." *

The Toleration Act was entitled "An Act for exempting their Majesties' Protestant subjects Dissenting from the Church of England from the penalties of certain laws. It thus introduced a new name for the Nonconformists namely PROTESTANT DISSENTERS, and by this name (and not Presbyterian or Independent) the Trust deeds of the chapels built under its protection designated the worshippers. The

* Somerset House Large folios, *Returns*, Vol. VIII., *Boroughs*.

Act expressly excluded from its benefits Roman Catholics and deniers of the doctrine of the blessed Trinity. No place of worship therefore could have been built under its protection by Unitarians. Presbyterians and Independents in rivalry during the Commonwealth had been brought to concord by a common persecution, and the two Denominations in and about London resolved to adopt the name *The United Brethren* under certain *Heads of Agreement* comprising such principles as both could agree to subscribe. This procedure was followed by several counties, and by the wholesome influence of Richard Baxter it found in Worcestershire a congenial soil. Thus it came to pass that in the Angel Street church-documents the designation Presbyterian is interchanged with Congregational. The church-government and discipline however, were evidently, and from the first, simply Congregational.

The Pastor, Thomas Badland, was assisted for some years after the drawing up and signing of the Church Covenant, by the young minister who came to Worcester in 1688, and who succeeded him, CHEWNING BLACKMORE.[*] Mr. Badland died May 5, 1698, and was buried in the chancel of old St. Martin's Church. "On a monument fixed to the south wall of the south aisle of St. Martin's Church," says Nash, "is the following inscription":—

Under these seats lies interred the body of the Rev. Mr. THOMAS BADLAND, *a faithful and profitable preacher*

---

[*] Account of C. Blackmore by Geo. Benson ; Blackmore MSS., Dr. Williams's Lib.

of the Gospel in this city for 35 *years.   He rested from his labours, May* 5, *A.D.* 1698, *ætat.* 64.
Mors mihi vita nova.

When St. Martin's Church was pulled down in 1768, the marble tablet which recorded his name was, with the rest of the building materials, thrown carelessly aside, and broken in many fragments.   These were discovered and purchased by a Trustee of the chapel, and, "the tablet was repaired at the expense of the congregation, and erected in the vestibule of Angel Street Chapel, where we trust it will long remain."   It did remain there till the chapel was taken down, and it is now erected near the pulpit in the present chapel.

There is extant a "Sermon preached at the funeral of Mr. Thomas Badland, a Nonconforming Minister at Kedderminster, by R. White, B.D., and Vicar of Kedderminster, London, 1693."   "The following discourse was delivered before a numerous congregation both of ministers and people, both Conformists and Nonconformists, about the beginning of February last.   R. WHITE, August 22, 1693."   Each leaf of this Sermon bears at the head these words, "A Sermon preached at the funeral of Mr. Thomas Badland."   But Thomas Badland was still living at this date and did not die for five years after.   Moreover, he was never minister at Kidderminster.   Furthermore, the description given of the minister is inappropriate to Mr.

Badland ;—speaking of his suffering from two diseases, the
stone and the gout, and of " his being a long time withheld
from the public exercise of his ministry," also of "that
reverend person" (meaning Ri. Baxter), "under whose
conduct he was when he came first to be an inhabitant of
the town." In Palmer's Nonconformist Memorial* the
sermon is rightly taken as having reference to THOMAS
BALDWIN of Chaddesley, who, after his ejectment, settled
with the Dissenters of Kidderminster, and of whom Baxter
says, " he had been our schoolmaster." Thos. Baldwin died
in Feb. 1693, and he clearly is the minister described. The
name *Badland* has been printed in mistake for *Baldwin*.

2.—The Rev. CHEWNING BLACKMORE.

1688–1737.

Chewning Blackmore was the son of a worthy nonconforming minister, the Rev. William Blackmore, of St.
Peter's, Cornhill, M.A., of Lincoln College, Oxford, ordained by Prideaux, Bishop of Worcester, and granted
Presbyterian orders from the Classis, and chosen Scribe to
the Provincial Presbyterian Assembly in London.† His
wife's name was Mary Chewning.

---

* Vol. III. p. 389.

† William Blackmore was minister at Pentlow, Essex, in Dec. 1645, a cure which he
resigned in 1646, and was succeeded by Henry Esday. He was one of sixty ministers who
petitioned Cromwell to show no violence to the king. He was involved in Love's plot, but

"William Blackmore and Mary Chewning were lawfully married in our parish church of Mary, Islington, May 1, 1660. William Barber, clerke of Mary, Islington."

"1662-3, Jan. 2. Baptized Chewning ye sonne of Mr. William Blackmore and Mary his wife; born the 1st of January."

Chewning Blackmore was at school (1672) under John Benson, M.A., of Peter House, Camb. (nonconforming minister of Little Leighs) at Writtle, in Essex. He was afterwards at school at Newington Green. Thence he went to Oxford in preparation for the ministry, and the Rev. Henry Cornish of Oxford gave him a testimonial dated April 18, 1688, describing him as "an unblemished and spiritually accomplished member of the small congregation in Oxon, to which I bear pastoral relation." * The Rev. George Benson in a funeral sermon from Heb. xiii., 7, gives the following account :—

"In the beginning of the year 1688, he came to this city (Worcester). He was, at first, assistant to good old Mr. Badland (who was also one that maintained his regard for the cause we espouse) in a very iniquitous time, and when it was dangerous to be so. Upon Mr. Badland's death he became pastor of this church, and how well qualified he was for the office, and with what constancy, diligence, and success he was

was released by Cromwell at the intercession of his brother. He was at St. Peter's, Cornhill, from 1649 to his ejectment for Nonconformity in 1662. He retired into Essex. In April 1672 he was licensed to be a Presb. Teacher in his own house, and his house was licensed to be a Presb. meeting-place. The house is described as in Home-Church. He was buried at Romford, Essex, 18 July, 1684. *See* David's *Nonc. in Essex*, 599, and *Pedigree of the Blackmore Family*, by Charles E. Blackmore Bowker, in Dr. Williams' Lib.

* Ch. Blackmore MSS. as before, Dr. Williams' Lib.

employed in the duties of it, many of you can tell from long experience.

It may, I think, be said of him that he was a person of a sedate, serene, and I might say somewhat reserved temper, one of great gravity in the pulpit and out of it.   His presence had an awe with it wherever he came, and there seemed to be an authority in his whole carriage.   .   .   His piety was observable every day and in his whole conduct ; he was a man of prayer and in devotion constant.

The matter of his preaching was spiritual and practical ; he preached Christ and Him crucified much, and the peculiar doctrines of the gospel revelation.   But practical religion lay near his heart, and was his most constant theme.

He was the father of our Denomination in this part of the island, and was one way or other concerned for many other churches besides his own ; and he was long an ornament to his function and a credit and support to the Dissenting interest ; for that cause he always shewed a most steady regard, and no one can well give a greater testimony of it than by designing most of his sons for the ministry, and actually educating two of them (as he did) in that way.   He thought that Nonconformity was built on the most stable principles, and it was his settled judgment that a further reformation is really necessary, in order to a more general and effectual reaching the great ends of Christianity.   This was our ancestors' opinion long ago. His behaviour towards young ministers was kind and obliging. He was very exact in governing his family.

This was the man whose excellent ministry and service this congregation enjoyed for 47 years.   For the last three years of his life he endured a grievous failure.   He died Aug. 2, 1737, in the 75th year of his age."

In 1694 he married ABIGAIL, daughter of Edward Higgins and Alice (née Franks) his wife, of Worcester, members of the church. Abigail was born 1676, married 1694, died 21 April, 1734.

Their children were :—

    1. Abigail, born and baptized Aug. 23, 1695. She was wife to Rev. Joseph Mottershead, minister of Cross Street Chapel, Manchester, who was born at Godley, 17 Aug. 1688, and died 4 Nov. 1771, aged 83. Buried at Cross Street Chapel, Manchester.

    2. William, born and baptized July 15, 1697.

    3. John, born March 30, baptized April 4, 1700.

    4. Francis, born April 18, baptized April 27, 1703.

    5. Edward Chewning, born Dec. 15, baptized Jan. 1, 1704 5. A son, stillborn, Nov. 2, 1708.

    6. Mary, born Sept. 14, 1709, baptized Oct. 14.

    7. Sarah, born June 9, 1711, baptized June 20.

The following letter shows the esteem in which Chewning Blackmore was held by his brethren in Worcestershire :—

Kidderminster, Mar. 24, 1706-7. Address of Worcestershire Ministers to Rev. Ch. B., entreating him to remain in Worcester, when invited to London.

DEAR AND HONOURED BROTHER.—We have been considering together your invitation to London, and what you have proposed to some of us who have spoken with you, both for and against your removal ; we hope you'll give us leave to represent our thoughts of the whole. We own if the choice was unanimous it is the more inviting, and worldly advantages are much greater there for ministers than in the country ;

they may not meet with so much opposition from people of
contrary opinions, and may have greater friends to stand by
them in such cases; we know also your field will be much
larger to work in; ministers there may be very desirous of
your company, you may have better opportunities for the well-
educating of your children; and we fear your people at Worcester have not been so encouraging as they ought to be.

Yet notwithstanding all this, we judge your removal may
have greater inconveniences attending it than these advantages
can answer.   We cannot think you can be so much desired by
a people that know you not at London, as we are sure you are
by the people you are with at Worcester.   Your worldly advantages are less where you are, yet your circumstances we hope
are not strait, and the blessing of God can enrich yours as well
as it hath done you.   Because of the difficulties we meet with
from opposers we can by no means be reconciled to let you go;
your knowledge of our countrey and circumstances make you
in many public respects the most capable person in encouraging,
advising, and many wayes assisting; should the most worthy
man succeed you, he cannot fill your place for many years,
because of his ignorance of our countrey and circumstances.
That place will much easier be filled than yours; how will adver-
saries triumph and reproach? Your people languish and divi-
sions break forth among them, your assistants mourn, your
brethren about lament, and the countrey round be greatly dis-
tressed, who are oft speaking to us with great concern! We
therefore humbly request you would consider it so as to resolve
you will continue among us; we would not meddle in your matter
but that the publick welfare and loss of the countrey depends upon
it.   Now our fathers in the ministry are gone, you are in their
stead to most of us hereabouts, and do not desert us dear Sir!

May we in anything be capable of serving you or your interest we shall rejoice to do it if you will stay with us. We know you are more able to give advice yourself than we to instruct you ; but yet we could not but show our thoughts. May God direct and prosper you is the prayer of

> Your unworthy Brethren and Servants,
>
> > JOHN SPILSBURY [of Kidderminster].
> >
> > EDWD. OSLAND [of Bewdley, see Toulmin 561].
> >
> > JAMES THOMPSON [of Broomsgrove ,, ,,].
> >
> > GEO. FLOWER [of Stourbridge].*
> >
> > RI. PRUTHERO.†
> >
> > JAMES SPILSBURY.‡
>
> Kidderminster, March 24, 1706-7."

The Rev. Chewning Blackmore had an assistant, Mr. HAND (Jonathan) who continued for some years, and whose

---

* GEORGE FLOWER, of Stourbridge, was a native of Burton-on-Trent, and pupil of Mr. Woodhouse at Sheriff Hales, was also chaplain to PHILIP FOLEY, of Prestwood. The Foleys were strong supporters of Protestant Dissenters. Chewning Blackmore had been tutor to Thomas, son of Paul Foley, Speaker of the House of Commons. In 1715 the interior of the Stourbridge meeting-house was sacked by a High-church mob. An "account of the damages done in the Riots of 1715, according to the several estimates returned by the Commissioners appointed by the King to enquire into them, 1716," states, "Stourbridge Meeting, £130 4s. 1d. ; Dudley Meeting, £304 12s. 4d." G. Flower died Jan. 1, 1733, aged 59 years, and was buried at Burton-on-Trent.

† RICE PRUTHERO, son of an ejected minister in South Wales, was educated at Abergavenny under Mr. Griffith. (Samuel Jones, afterwards the celebrated tutor of Tewkesbury, studied at the same academy.) He was ordained June, 1702, and Matthew Henry, who took part, speaks of him as of Bragginton, Montgomery. *The Blackmore Papers,* by R. Brooke Aspland, p. 32.

‡ JAMES SPILSBURY was educated at Tewkesbury under SAMUEL JONES, who had a famous academy there from 1708 till his death in 1719, Bp. Butler, Archb. Secker, Chandler, being students. In the list John Spilsbury is described as "attorney-at-law"; but he evidently became a Worcestershire minister. New. Coll. Hist. Library, *Wilson Memorials,* I. fol. 27.

name occurs in the Baptismal Register occasionally down
to 1713.   He was educated for the ministry at Sheriff Hales,
and ordained in Oldbury Chapel, Staffordshire on May 30,
1699, with three others, John Reynolds, of Gloucester,
Shrewsbury, and Walsall, Warren of Coventry, and Bennet.
Mr. Mansfield prayed over Mr. Hand, who came to Worcester.*   The usual religious services were continued, and
in addition to the mode of admitting communicants, dates
were added to the respective signatures.   This was continued
through the whole of Mr. Blackmore's life.   The number
of names with dates affixed is 251.   Among these only two
now remain connected with the congregation, THOMAS
BLACKWELL, June 15, 1721, and GEORGE GILLAM, Feb. 14,
1723.   JOHN HODGES and SARAH HODGES, Apr. 17, 1735,
are the last signatures except two, Mrs. ELIZABETH HODGES,
our late respected friend, being the last survivor of a family
connected with the congregation from its reorganization in
1687.   After Mr. Hand's death,† Mr. JOHN BUTLER, at that
time a celebrated printer in Worcester, was employed to
invite Mr. JOHN STOKES, who then resided with his father
in Dudley, to become assistant to Mr. Blackmore.   Mr.
Stokes accepted the invitation.   After some time he married
Penelope Hand, whose name appears June 19, 1722, commenced as schoolmaster, and kept his school in the chapel,

---

* *Life of John Reynolds,* 1735, pp. 25, 26.

† Mr. Hand died in December 1719, and John Stokes came the following year.
Morrice MSS., Dr. Williams's Lib.   Mr. Blackmore appears to have lodged with Butler
previous to his marriage.   Afterwards he lived in "Powick Lane."

till from injuries done to the building he was obliged to remove the school elsewhere. He never would be ordained, but continued to assist Mr. Blackmore and others till an unfortunate disagreement caused him to remove from Worcester. His refusing ordination prevented his becoming a Pastor. He lived to the advanced age of 86, and died at his son's home at *the Rhydd*, now the seat of Sir Anthony Lechmere, Bart.

The Place of Worship in Angel Street was built in 1708, and was registered at the Quarter Sessions as a place of worship for the Presbyterians. In the riots, which took place in 1715, when many meeting-houses were destroyed, it was considered in so much danger that for some weeks a watch was kept for its preservation. In that year one of the church-members, THOMAS YARDLEY, was Mayor of Worcester, and the Corporation did him the honour of escorting him to the Chapel, and left him at the door. The bigotry prevailing in that day is not yet extinct; but among the great Evangelical party in the Establishment a more liberal feeling is cherished.

Mr. Blackmore built the back part of the last North-east house in Foregate Street, furnished his parlour with a large collection of portraits of Nonconformist Ministers, which was considered quite a curiosity, and as such was frequently visited by Sir C. Trubshaw Withers. Mr. Blackmore died

July 15, 1737, and was buried in St. Andrew's Church,
where a monument to his memory remains.   He left £40
for the poor of the congregation, £60 to be put to interest
for the distribution of BIBLES, and the interest of £50 for
preaching two sermons annually to young people on July 15
(the birthday of his father), and on New Year's Day.   The
subjects to be *the danger of delay in religion*, and *the
power and grace of Christ*.   In a statistical record in the
Morrice MSS. the number of hearers during Mr. Blackmore's ministry is stated to have been 700.

Chewning Blackmore was a close student of Holy
Scripture.   But he carried into his pulpit discourses something beside the book knowledge of the scholar ; he was an
habitual student of the human heart.   He excelled especially
in prayer.   His example in respect to the impressiveness,
aptness of phrase, variety and earnest spirituality of his
prayers, was used by a contemporary as a defence of ex-
tempore prayer.   His style of address was popular, and he
abstained from controversial topics in the pulpit.   His
manners were dignified ; his pastoral visits were systematic,
though brief.   The cause of Protestant Nonconformity he
upheld firmly and with dignity.   In the year after Mr.
Blackmore's settlement, EDWARD STILLINGFLEET was pro-
moted to the see of Worcester, and in his primary charge
he instructed his clergy to seek the acquaintance of Dissenters in order to do them good.   But, soon after, he

intimated to the Dissenters that if, through the Indulgence they grew " more headstrong and insolent," he would have them take notice they would make themselves liable to the law. Dr. Calamy remarks, "This is a plain intimation he was not desirous the Dissenters should have too much liberty. Nor was this peculiar to him ; it was the common temper of the clergy towards them." *

3.—REV. FRANCIS SPILSBURY.

1737-1744.

He was grandson of JOHN SPILSBURY, fellow of Magdalen College, Oxon, and minister of Bromsgrove during the Commonwealth, who married the sister of Dr. Joseph Hall, Bishop of Bristol, by whom he had a son of the same name, many years pastor of a congregation at Kidderminster. John Spilsbury, the grandfather, resigned his living in 1662 for conscience sake, and continuing his ministry privately amongst his people, he was once imprisoned in the county jail, where the want of air and exercise laid the foundation of that illness which brought him to the grave. He died June 10, 1699, aged 71 years. The son, John Spilsbury, junior, nephew, executor and

* *Blackmore Papers,* by R. Brooke Aspland, pp. 27, 28.

heir of Bishop Hall, was for 33 years pastor of the Kidderminster Church, and died in 1727.   His son, Francis Spilsbury, was born at Kidderminster in 1706, and was placed
for the ministry under the tuition of Dr. Ebenezer Latham,
at Findern, Derbyshire. He completed his collegiate
studies at Glasgow, attending the Lectures of Professor
Simpson.   Returning to Kidderminster after his father's
death he became assistant to his father's successor, Matthew
Bradshaw, and thence he removed to Bromsgrove as successor to an excellent minister, the Rev. James Thompson.
Here his ministry was highly appreciated.   Upon the death
of Chewning Blackmore he accepted the invitation of the
church in Angel Street to become their pastor, 1737, and remained seven years.   He was acceptable, popular and useful.
He had the offer of a good living in the Establishment,
at Ashby-de-la-Zouch, in Leicestershire, but he firmly and
promptly rejected the proposal.*   Being urged to come
to London to be co-pastor with the Rev. John Barker at
Salter's Hall, he settled in London, and his life was pro-
longed to a good old age.   He died March 3, 1782, in the
77th year of his age.   He was a man of amiable character.
He was firmly attached to the doctrines of grace, and was
Baxterian in his theology.   He kept up his connection with
Worcester by an annual visit, at which time he preached
and conducted a series of public services.

* Worthington's *Sermon on the death of Francis Spilsbury*, pp. 22-24.   Toulmin's *History of Dissenters*, p. 561.

4.—The Rev. FRANCIS BLACKMORE.

1744, 1745.

Francis Blackmore and his brother Edward Chewning Blackmore were received with others to Communion, June 15, 1721. Francis, after his studies for the ministry, was ordained as the successor of the Rev. Daniel Higgs, minister at Evesham, who died in October, 1728. Next he became assistant to John Warren,* of Coventry, and on the removal of Mr. Spilsbury was invited to succeed him as pastor, Mr. Stokes continuing Assistant. " This connexion too soon became so very unfortunate that the elders and managers expelled Mr. Blackmore, who, on a Lord's Day morning, finding the pulpit occupied by Mr. Adams, of Bewdley, left the place instantly and never entered it afterwards, yet never resigned or would give up his claim to be pastor as long as he lived. He resided in the house in Foregate Street till his death in the year 1760, and was buried in St. Andrew's Church, where some account of him still remains.† Mr.

---

* John Warren was one of Mr. Woodhouse's pupils. He was chaplain to Philip Foley, of Prestwood, near Kidderminster, and thence went to be assistant to Mr. Tong at Coventry, then as co-pastor with Joshua Merrel, and then as sole pastor, till his death in 1742. Toulmin's *His. of Dissenters*, 562.

† St. Andrew's, "South Ile, at the east end.—FRANCIS BLACKMORE, A.M., *obiit die vigesimo Decembris*, A.D. 1760.—Rev. EDWARD CHEWNING BLACKMORE [minister of Stoke-upon-Severn], died Nov. 1st, 1787, aged 82. A neat marble monument near this place of the family sepulture, was put up for the father, CHEWNING BLACKMORE, and his wife, ABIGAIL, in 1741, with a Latin inscription." Valentine Green's *History of Worcester*, Vol. II., Appendix, p. 108. Edward Chewning Blackmore lived in Worcester unmarried, amid a fine collection of books, and rode over to Stoke on Sundays. He jocularly observed that he never received as much for preaching as kept his horse.

H

Stokes immediately withdrew from Worcester and became
minister to a small congregation at Ledbury, but for some
years before his death resided in Worcester or its vicinity."
Francis Blackmore is described as "a man of refined tastes
and religious spirit, of rational piety, and great devotion,
free from any undue attachments to the opinions of men in
the affairs of religion." He married Mary, daughter of
Robert Wilkes of Bromsgrove, by whom he had issue two
daughters and a son named William Wilkes Blackmore,
who settled in business in Manchester.*

> During Mr. Francis Blackmore's time serious disagreements
> had arisen between the managers of the congregation and the
> Corporation.   The ground upon which the present (1841)
> building stands was the property of Mr. Timothy Colles, whose
> name appears in the Register of members Feb. 18, 1703.   The
> usual renewable lease from the Corporation for 41 years was
> made to him of a garden with the " Blanquet " or " Banquett-
> ing-house " thereon, in 1708, the year in which the chapel was
> erected.   The lease was again renewed to the same Timothy
> Colles, and under the same description in 1722; which lease
> was never renewed, and of course expired in 1763.   The dis-
> agreement above alluded to having increased, the present
> building and premises were sold to Rowland Priddy and Jos.
> Priddy for the understood and avowed purpose of converting
> the present building into a playhouse, and the Corporation
> executed a lease dated June 2, 1740, to those persons for the
> usual term of 41 years, but to commence from Michaelmas, 1763,
> the time the lease was to expire.   To prevent this, two leading

* *Blackmore Papers*, pp. 61, 63.

men of the congregation, RICHARD BROAD and PHILIP FINCHER, Esq. of Shell, purchased, with property belonging to the congregation, freehold premises in Mealcheapen Street, intending to take down and remove all the building except the " Banquetting House," and leave the ground as a garden just as it was before 1708 ; intending to build another Meeting House on the freehold property in Mealcheapen Street. This becoming probably known, proved so offensive to the late Alderman Johnson, whose dwelling house adjoined the freehold, and who did not like a Presbyterian Meeting at his next door, that a final arrangement was made that the premises should be held under the lease to the Priddys for the first fourteen years of their renewable lease ; that it should be afterwards renewed for the congregation at a fine of £31 10s., and a nominal rent of 2s. and capons. It was consequently so held till a new lease was granted for 41 years, renewable as usual every fourteen years, from Michaelmas 1777, to fifteen persons therein named, upon the reserved rent, usual covenants, and renewable fine of £31 10s. This was the first lease ever granted to trustees ; and of these fifteen persons the late Mr. T. Hodges was the indisputable survivor. The lease has ever since been regularly renewed, under the same description, and in the same terms in the years 1791, 1805, 1819, and 1833. The present trustees have now (1841) consented to the proposed terms for enfranchising the same under the late Municipal Reform Act. During Mr. Blackmore's time also Mrs. Sarah Carter left a leasehold house in Foregate Street for the dwelling of the ministers ; it has, however, been long since sold.*

In 1743 ISAAC MADDOX, who attacked the Puritan historian, DANIEL NEAL, became Bishop of Worcester, as

* From Samuel Blackwell's MS., written 1841.

successor to the beloved JOHN HOUGH. In childhood a pastrycook's boy, Maddox was sent, by an exhibition of some Dissenting friends, to college at Aberdeen.* But, entering the Establishment, he was made curate of St. Bride's, and after other promotions, Bishop of St. Asaph in 1736; and, in November 1743, was translated to Worcester; he died in 1759. His strictures upon Neal's *History of the Puritans,* were fully answered by Neal himself in his *Review of the principal facts objected to,* and by JOSHUA TOULMIN, in notes to his edition of Neal's great work in 5 volumes, 8vo, 1822, in which he also refutes the objections of Zachary Grey and William Warburton, Bishop of Gloucester.

5.—The Rev. JOSEPH CARPENTER.

1744–1760.

(THOMAS URWICK, Assistant.)

Soon after the lamentable disagreement referred to, the Rev. Joseph Carpenter, of Warwick, was invited to officiate, and accepting the invitation became the acknowledged pastor. He must, however, have known all the pre-existent circumstances. He expressed surprise that the Congregation should invite so old a man, but said, if they grew tired and

* John Chambers' *Biographical Illustrations of Worcestershire,* p. 356.

wished a change, they would not have much trouble in getting rid of him. The Rev. THOMAS URWICK became his Assistant in the year 1754. Mr. Carpenter was much esteemed. He resided in the house left for the minister till his death about the year 1760. He is supposed to have been buried at Bromsgrove. He and Mr. Francis Blackmore seem to have died about the same time.

Joseph Carpenter pursued his academical studies at Alcester in Warwickshire, under Mr. Joseph Porter, from whom many gentlemen merchants and ministers received their education. In the year 1715 he was settled at Warwick, and continued there till 1744, when he removed to Worcester to succeed Mr. Blackmore as pastor of the Presbyterian congregation. His removal to this place gave him, in the review, great satisfaction, and in a letter, dated Oct. 3, 1752, he says, "Surely, if ever any one was under a particular direction, I was in that affair." Mr. Carpenter spent the rest of his days in this connection, and died about the year 1758. He published two sermons, one on occasion of a fast, and another preached at Coventry, Sept. 19, 1742, upon the death of the Rev. John Warren, from 1 John, iv., 16. Several of Mr. Carpenter's letters to Mr. John Ward, of Taunton, appeared in the Protestant Dissenters' Magazine for August, 1798, vol. 5, p. 283 289. He married, and left a daughter, who became wife to Wm. Kettle, of Birmingham, who left a son and two daughters,

the youngest of whom became wife to Rev. John Kentish
of Birmingham.   Mr. Carpenter had a brother, John Carpenter, of Woodrow, near Bromsgrove, from whom des-
cended the late Benjamin Carpenter of Bromsgrove, and
Dr. Lant Carpenter, who were first cousins.*

6.—The Rev. John Allen, M.D.

1760–1764.

(Thomas Urwick, Assistant.)

The Rev. John Allen, M.D., of London, accepted an
invitation to succeed Mr. Carpenter, Mr. Urwick continuing
Assistant.   He resided when at Worcester in the minister's
house in Foregate Street.   He was a pupil of Samuel
Jones at Tewkesbury.   He had first been settled for a
short time at Nailsworth in Gloucestershire, whence he
removed to London in the autumn of 1730, to succeed
Dr. John Evans as co-pastor with Mr. James Read in the
congregation in New Broad Street, Petty-France.   He
had for many years a large and substantial congregation,
and made a handsome collection for the fund.   He was a
highly respectable man, a good, judicious preacher, and in
his religious sentiments a moderate Calvinist.   Besides his
stated services in his own congregation, he was for some

* W. Wilson's *Biog. Coll.*, I. 338.

THE REV. THOMAS URWICK,

Minister of Angel Street Church, 1764 1775.

From a portrait in Pastels in the Coward Trustees' Room, New College, Hampstead.)

years afternoon preacher to the congregation in Hanover Street under the ministry of the aged Dr. Earle. He was also one of the preachers of the Thursday Lecture in the same place. Dr. Allen was at Worcester from 1760 to 1764, when he resigned his charge and retired to London. He died Dec. 31, 1774, in the 73rd year of his age, and his remains were interred in Bunhill Fields, where a flat stone is raised over his grave, which contains the following inscription :—

The Reverend Doctor Allen
who departed this life, December 31st, 1774,
In the 73rd year of his age.
"Well done thou good and faithful servant."

He was some time with the Independent Church at Shrewsbury.*

7.—The Rev. THOMAS URWICK.

1764–1775.

THOMAS URWICK,† the second son of Samuel Urwick,‡ was born December 8, 1727, at Shelton, near Shrewsbury,

* *History of Diss. Churches*, II. 225; Dr. Williams's Lib., W. Wilson's *Biog. Coll.*, I. 14.

† Abridged from the Walter Wilson MSS., M. 4, in Dr. Williams's Library; endorsed, "From the Rev. THOS. TAYLOR, of Carter Lane, who furnished me with this account when I was writing *The Dissenting Churches*, in 1809. WALTER WILSON."

‡ SAMUEL URWICK owned a small estate of about 400 acres at Shelton, which he farmed. He was a Nonconformist, and nephew to EDWARD URWICK, B.A., incumbent of Eastham from 1690 till his death in 1701, and master of Tenbury School. (Nash, I. 367). On the

where he received his classical education.   Discovering a strong inclination to the Christian ministry, and encouraged by the Rev. JOB ORTON (on whose ministry his parents were constant attendants), he entered, in 1747, the college at Northampton, under Doctor Doddridge.   After Doddridge's death he went to Glasgow in 1752, where he finished his academical studies under Dr. Leechman.   "In 1754 he received a unanimous invitation from the congregation at Worcester, under the pastoral care of Mr. CARPENTER, to assist him in his growing infirmities.   Upon Mr. Carpenter's death in 1758, the congregation wished him to fill the vacant office, but this he declined; and Dr. ALLEN, though advanced in years, was invited from London and induced to accept it ; Mr. Urwick at ye same time agreed to become his assistant, and frequently preached both parts of ye day, and sometimes for two or three months together without any pecuniary reward for his extra services.   Dr. Allen's infirmities increasing with his age, he resigned ye charge in 1764, and Thomas Urwick was unanimously chosen as his successor. The duties of ye office which he had now undertaken he

blank pages of the Register book of St. Juliana, Shrewsbury, now in the *Shrewsbury Free Library*, there are several notices of baptisms in Nonconformist families, such as, "Thomas, son of JOB ORTON and Mary his wife, *said to be* by an Independent Teacher, baptised Sept. 11, 1721."   Again, "May 27, 1723, Mary, d. of Job and Mary ORTON *said to be* baptised by Mr. BERRY a Dissenting Teacher."   There are also notices of the whole family of Samuel Urwick, "Farmer in Shelton," who were "*said to be* baptised" by Mr. BERRY. The Rev. Charles Berry was assistant to Dr. JOHN GYLES at Shrewsbury from 1721, and after Dr. Gyles's death in 1730 he continued sole minister till his death in 1741, when JOB ORTON succeeded.   Dr. ALLEN and CH. BERRY were fellow students under SAMUEL JONES at Tewkesbury.   *Wilson Memorials,* I. 27, New Coll. Hist. Lib.

discharged with so much acceptance and usefulness, that few ministers were ever more beloved by their hearers. And in this situation it is probable he would have continued to ye day of his death, had not circumstances arisen which he thought required his removal; an event which took place in ye year 1775. The two or three following years he spent among his friends, and in looking about for some retired situation where he might end his days. With this view he accepted an invitation from a small congregation in ye village of *Narborough*,* near Leicester, and here he thought to have found what he had been seeking. But ye great Lord and Head of ye Church would not suffer a servant so well fitted for advancing his glory to remain in ye obscurity in which he wished himself to be buried, and in ye year 1779 he received an invitation from ye congregation at Clapham to fill ye vacancy which ye much lamented removal of their excellent pastor, Dr. FURNEAUX, had occasioned. This important office, after serious deliberation he thought it his duty to accept, and here, as in his former situation, he made full proof of his ministry till ye infirmities of age disabled him for stated services; occasional ones he still continued cheerfully to perform, frequently for Mr. PHILIPPS,† his worthy successor, and sometimes for other of

* Thos. Urwick succeeded THOMAS HIRONS (brother of Jabez Hirons of St. Albans) as minister of Narborough and Great Wigston in June 1776, and remained there till 1778. See Non-parochial Registers in Somerset House, Leicestershire, 43, 1.

† JAMES PHILIPPS was assistant and successor to Thos. Urwick in the Clapham pastorate. He was here 23 years, and died here May 14, 1824, aged 64 years. He was one of the Coward Trustees from 1815 till his death. He in turn was followed by the Rev. G. BROWN.

his brethren. It was always, and in every situation that Providence allotted him, his great delight, in humble imitation of his Divine Master, to go about doing good. This was a prominent feature in his amiable character ; and he spared no pains, but often put himself to greater fatigue and inconvenience than his friends wished, to accomplish his benevolent purposes." *

"The great and distinguishing truths of the Christian faith, and those particularly which serve to exalt the grace of God as it is exercised and displayed to sinful men through the Sacrifice and Mediation of Christ Jesus, were the favourite subjects of his meditation, and ran through his sermons and his prayers." †

Upon Mr. Urwick's acceptance of the full pastorate at Worcester, an ordination service was held. The ministers

* For example :—Visiting in Clapham, one Monday morning, he entered a shop, where he found a poor mother in deep grief because her son had disappeared from home, and had gone, she feared, to enlist in the Navy. Mr. Urwick comforted her by saying that he knew the Admiral, and would write to him. In due time the boy was found, having already gone on board ship ; but through Mr. Urwick's influence he was sent back with money to pay his journey. This youth was none other than the afterwards celebrated JOSEPH LANCASTER, the founder of the *British* or *Lancasterian* system of education. *Monthly Repository*, ii. 161 (1807) ; *Gentleman's Magazine*, 1807, p. 282 ; *Sketches*, part I., *Joseph Lancaster*, by Henry Dunn ; London, 1848, 24mo.

† Mr. Urwick published a sermon on the death of his friend, the Rev. HUGH FARMER, regarding whom he writes, " He expressed great consolation from the promises of the Gospel, and the covenant of mercy which was sealed by the blood of Christ. We must always," continues Mr. Urwick in this Sermon, " *look for the mercy* of our Lord Jesus Christ unto eternal life." Also in 1785 a Sermon on Psalm 119, v. 9 ; and in 1800, a Sermon entitled, *The proper improvement of Divine Chastening, recommended to National Attention ;* preached at Clapham by THOS. URWICK, March 12, 1800. 8vo. Cadell junior and Davies. "A plain, serious, and useful discourse"; *Monthly Review*, New Series, Vol. 33, p. 334.

taking part were Benjamin Faucett, of Kidderminster, who offered the ordination prayer, Mr. Wyld, of Carr's Lane Meeting, Birmingham, Francis Spilsbury, of London, John Stokes, of Ledbury. Mr. Urwick married Miss Smith, a descendant of the Elder, THOMAS SMITH. He never resided in the minister's house, but after his marriage in a house of his own, as long as he continued in Worcester. The Lord's Supper was administered every month; the young were regularly catechised, Sabbath by Sabbath,—the youngest in Dr. Watts's catechism, the elder in the Assembly's. When Thomas Urwick accepted the pastorate he stated in an affectionate letter, "it is upon my heart to live and to die with you." The congregation, therefore, were surprised and grieved when he announced his intention to leave Worcester. He had been with them as Assistant and Pastor 21 years, from 1754 to 1775. Much was said to induce him to change his intentions, but "his strong determination to leave Worcester" (to use the late Job Orton's expression) was fixed, and he took an affectionate farewell in a sermon from Matt. xxviii. 20. He was for many years a Trustee of Dr. Williams's Library, and also of Coward College. He died Feb. 26, 1807, and was buried on the north side of the churchyard of Clapham Church. On his tomb is this Inscription : —

"Here are deposited the mortal remains of the Rev. THOMAS URWICK, during twenty-six years the able, faithful and beloved Pastor of the Protestant Dissenting Church in the parish. He was born December 8, 1727, and died after a short confinement, on the 26th day of February, in the year 1807. Here also are deposited the remains of his wife, MARY URWICK, who departed this life the 17th June, 1791, aged sixty-five years."

"The late Mr. TAYLOR of Carter Lane * was applied to after Mr. Urwick's departure from Worcester, and was invited, but declined acceptance. Next, Mr. HALLIDAY preached three Sabbaths, but he also declined ; and a long period intervened before a Pastor could be chosen. Soon after Mr. Urwick settled at Clapham, he addressed a very kind and friendly letter to the congregation, expressing his wish to serve them. He said :—

"I know you want a serious, affectionate and evangelical minister, and I am looking out for such a one for you. Keep of one mind. Never think of having more than one candidate at one time. Cultivate such a spirit of affectionate union, as will enable me to say the most lovely things concerning you." He also recommended altering the mode of invitation,—which had been sent to Mr. Taylor and Mr. Halliday by the managers only,—and to let it be by the managers, members in fellowship, and subscribers generally. This was in future always adopted. Mr. Urwick had been left, by an old lady, Mrs. Sarah Carter, probably a relative of Hannah Carter, registered a communicant Aug. 11, 1720, the whole of her property only charged with an annuity for an old servant during her life. This Mr. Urwick purchased for her in one of the Public offices, and vested the remainder in the public Funds, for the congregation, thereby increasing their funded property by, at least, £1000, 3 per cent.

* MS. Narrative of Samuel Blackwell, written 1841.

consols. This money, we learn, was afterwards (1797) expended in building or improving the Vestry used as a Girls' schoolroom.

The late Job Orton, then residing at Kidderminster, introduced Mr. WARBURTON, formerly of Creaton, as a temporary supply. He came, and continued till Mr. Belsham was afterwards chosen. Two of the students from Daventry were favourites, THOMAS BELSHAM and GEORGE OSBORN, and they both afterwards successively became Pastors. During this interval a special PRAYER MEETING was commenced, and was held in the south end of the east gallery, then known as "the old praying seat." Liberty to use the vestry was then obtained, and meetings were held on Sunday mornings and Thursday evenings. The names of those who began it were John Hodges, Henry Bromley, Richard Barker, Martin Barr, Charles Berry, Thomas Berry, James Price, and the present writer, Samuel Blackwell. Benjamin Burden and James Mence afterwards joined. The present *City Library* now in Pierpoint Street was also first begun about this time by a few persons of the congregation. It was kept in a room in Angel Street; afterwards removed to a room over the vestry, where it continued till after the Library-building in Pierpoint Street was erected, where it still exists. The late Rev. John Stokes, having returned to Worcester, was very active in this business." *

Some time before Mr. Belsham's settlement, an attempt

* S. Blackwell's MS. Record, 1841.

was made to commence a separate interest, also called
Independent. After his departure it was for some time
continued. The Rev. JOHN LEWIS, afterwards of Wotton-
under-Edge, was minister. Dr. Edward Williams, when at
Ross, gave the movement some encouragement, and the
Rev. THOMAS WILLIAMS, of Hereford, was ordained there.
But after a few years it was finally abandoned, and the
building, or the ground on which it stood, is now occupied
by the METHODIST CHAPEL, Pump Street. See Registers
in the Appendix.

8.—The Rev. THOMAS BELSHAM, M.A.

1778–1781.

It having been determined by the leading members of
the congregation to wait the completion of Thomas
Belsham's studies at Daventry, he received an invitation,
and stated in his letter of acceptance, "My visit to Worcester confirms the opinion I had before entertained of the
candour of Mr. Urwick's congregation, and affords a
pleasing hope of that success in promoting the interest of
Christ and his religion, which is the grand object of my
most ardent desire." [*] He was son of an evangelical

[*] This extract is given in an interesting account of the Angel St. Church by Mr. RICHARD
EVANS, in the possession of Mr. T. Rowley Hill, an account often made use of in this
history.

minister at Newport Pagnell, and studied at Daventry.
He was ordained in Worcester on Oct. 9, 1778. In his
confession of faith on the occasion there was no indication
of any departure from orthodox belief. The Rev. Benjamin
Faucett, of Kidderminster, offered the ordination prayer,
accompanied with the imposition of hands of the ministers
present. The Rev. Thomas Taylor,* of Carter Lane
Meeting, London, preached, and Mr. WOOD, of Dudley,
asked the questions, and received the confession of faith.
Mr. Belsham's sermons were generally acceptable. After
one upon the subject of being "ashamed of Christ," Mr.
Belsham himself gave out the well known hymn :—

> " Jesus, and shall it ever be,
> A mortal man ashamed of Thee."

Persons wishing communion were admitted as heretofore ;
discipline was not neglected. This sufficiently proves that
Mr. Belsham had not while at Worcester embraced the
opinions which have since rendered his name so notorious,
and placed him at the head of the Socinian party. In
consequence of the retirement of THOMAS ROBBINS,† he
received an invitation in September, 1781, to become tutor,

* THOMAS TAYLOR was born in the neighbourhood of Kidderminster, and was a grandson of RICHARD SERJEANT, ejected from Stone. In early life he attended the ministry of
the pious and excellent BENJAMIN FAUCETT, with whom he contracted a lifelong friendship.
He was a student at Daventry under the learned CALEB ASHWORTH, successor of Doddridge.
He afterwards settled at Carter Lane.

† Born near Bedford. Attended the ministry of Mr. Saunderson ; studied under Doddridge ; settled at Stretton, Warwickshire ; afterwards at West Bromwich ; succeeded Dr.
Ashworth at Daventry.

which he accepted.   He preached his farewell sermon from Philip. i. 27.   As Daventry was supported by the Coward fund, bequeathed with the express condition that the students shall be educated in the principles of *the Assembly's Cate- chism*, when Mr. Belsham abandoned those principles for Socinianism he with great propriety relinquished the theolo- gical chair, and was succeeded by JOHN HORSEY,* of North- ampton.   Within ten years the Academy was dissolved.†

9.—The Rev. JOSEPH GUMMER.

1781–1791.

In November 1781, JOSEPH GUMMER, minister at Here- ford, and recommended by the Rev. Job Orton, was called to the pastorate.   The minister's house in Foregate Street, having been sold, he resided in part of what was afterwards Mr. Colville's school in Silver Street, till a parsonage adjoining the chapel was built for him.   Here he resided till he left Worcester.   During the first year of his ministry the congregation much increased ; from six to seven hundred generally attended.   He was respected by the neighbouring ministers.   He offered the ordination prayer at the ordination

* JOHN HORSEY was son of Rev. John Horsey, of Ringwood and Warminster ; he was educated at Homerton College, 1771-5.   In 1777 he became minister of Castle Hill, Northampton, and remained there fifty years.   He died May 12, 1827, aged 73 years. MS. Daventry Students, &c., *New Coll.*, Hampstead.

† Bogue and Bennett's *Hist. of Dissenters*, Vol. 4, pp. 269, 270.

THE REV. GEORGE OSBORN.

Minister of Angel Street Church, 1791—1812.

of George Osborn at West Bromwich, at which Dr. Addington took part. But the congregation declined, and means were resorted to, hardly less objectionable than those adopted in the case of Francis Blackmore, to induce him to resign ; he removed to Ilminster in Somerset (his native county). He was a most amiable man, and much respected by many, and especially by the youth of the congregation, but he was not an attractive preacher. After a lapse of twenty-eight years, in 1819, he visited Worcester again, and preached three Sundays. All were delighted to see his face again. These were his last public labours, he was called to his rest a year or two afterwards.*

10.—The Rev. George Osborn.

1791–1812.

On the 4th of November 1791, the Rev. George Osborn, of West Bromwich, accepted the invitation to the pastoral charge—an invitation, however, by no means unanimous, because he held Baptist views. He retained the office for nineteen years, till his death in 1812. Born in Cork, Nov. 13, 1757, a student at Daventry, ordained 1787, he was a faithful and able minister. He kept a boarding-school, on which he was in great degree dependent for the support of his family. Soon after his settlement as Pastor

---

* Mr. Ri. Evans' *MS. Account of the Angel Street Church*, in the possession of T. Rowley Hill, his son-in-law.

I

he proposed the formation of an *Evangelical Association* for the county, and a Meeting of Ministers was held at Kidderminster on Dec. 11, 1793, in Mr. Barrett's church, where Mr. Osborn preached from Philip. i. 27. At the meeting were present the Revs. HUNT of Stourbridge, DAWSON of Evesham, Geo. Osborn of Worcester, ROGERS of Bromsgrove, SMITH of Pershore, J. BARRETT of Kidderminster, LEWIS of Worcester. The Rev. J. Barrett was chosen *Moderator*, and resolutions were agreed to forming an Association of Ministers and Congregational Churches in the county of Worcester, who profess Calvinistic sentiments and admit of Free Communion. Mr. JOHN WATSON of Kidderminster was requested to act as Treasurer; the expenses of the Association to be defrayed by voluntary subscriptions.* On Aug. 14, 1799, they met again at Ledbury, as "*The Worcestershire and Herefordshire Union.*" Fourteen ministers attended, and Mr. Osborn was among the preachers. A United Prayer Meeting for the spread of the Gospel was begun this year in Worcester and held every month in Angel Street, Silver Street, and Birdport Chapels.†

Mr. Osborn was also the founder of the FIRST SUNDAY SCHOOL (in the modern sense) in the City of Worcester. He writes :—"Soon after coming to reside in Worcester, I noticed multitudes of poor, idle, miserable-looking children,

---

* *Evangelic Faith and Union, A Sermon on Philip.* i. 27, *preached at Kidderminster*, 11 *Dec.* 1793, *before the Association of Independent Churches of Worcestershire, and published by their desire.* By the Rev. GEORGE OSBORN. *Preface*, pp. iv.–vi.

† *Evangelical Magazine*, 1794. p. 216; 1790, p. 557.

sauntering and begging about the streets, it struck me that
Sunday Schools might help to prevent such a nuisance.
We commenced a Sunday School for boys, Aug. 20, 1797.
I preached for their benefit May 27, 1798, and through the
encouragement then afforded we established another school
for girls. In 1800 we were enabled to furnish the boys with
hats and girls with bonnets, visitors giving the girls tippets.
And this year, 1801, I can plead the cause of 130 poor
children who are now presented with a comfortable article
of dress each, and the most deserving are instructed in writing, &c., on the week-day evenings. They are freely taught
to read and believe the BIBLE; they are regularly brought
twice on the Lord's Day to public worship; they are also
instructed to repeat hymns, and to learn the catechisms of
WATTS and of the orthodox *Assembly of Divines* in which
they are examined publicly by the minister every month." *

"During the last seven years of his ministry the church was
much disturbed by financial difficulties. The number of Trustees
being reduced to five, the surviving Trustees executed an
additional DECLARATION OF TRUST, describing the congregation
to be ' Protestant Dissenters of the Presbyterian or Independent
Denomination professing the principles and practices described
in the *Assembly's Catechism* ; that the minister should be chosen
by the Members in fellowship, Trustees, and Subscribers ; that
the male members should vote with the Trustees in the choice
of one of the Trustees to be *Receiver*, and that all the produce

* From an *Address* prefixed to a *Sermon* preached in Angel Street Chapel on behalf of
the Sunday School by Rev. Gen. Osborn, Nov. 9, 1800. *See* Noake's *Worcester Sects*,
pp. 127, 128.

of the property and all subscriptions should, after deducting necessary expenses, be applied to the maintenance of the minister.' Messrs. RICHARD EVANS, STOKES, BURDEN, YOUNG, STEPHEN BURDEN, EDWARD EVANS and SAMUEL BLACKWELL did unanimously depute Messrs. RICHARD EVANS and SAMUEL BLACKWELL to wait upon Mr. GILLAM, and with him to settle everything necessary. This DEED being engrossed and duly executed was enrolled in Chancery, and expressly referred to in the Lease last made to the parties now holding it from the Corporation. The Trustees having agreed to accept the terms proposed, and to enfranchise the property, nothing more is necessary." Mr. Richard Evans writes : ' I have never seen cause to regret the part I took in that affair, nor did I ever hear a word of regret fall from any one who acted with us, except lamenting that it should have been necessary to spend so much of our own property in protecting the interest of this Christian Society." *

The following extract from the Rev. Thomas Urwick's Will throws light upon the pecuniary position of the church at this period :—

Whereas JOSEPH DOUGLAS, late of the city of Worcester, Gentleman, deceased, by his last Will and Testament, bearing date Nov. 2, 1791, gave in trust for the benefit of the Meeting House belonging to the Dissenting Congregation in Angel Street, in the city of Worcester, the sum of £300, and the further sum of £36 for the renewal of the lease of the said Meeting House, and the said two several sums were to be paid by his executors into my hands for the purposes aforesaid, but not to be applied for the benefit of Mr. Osborn, a Baptist Minister, if he were chosen minister of that place, but to remain in my hands, and to be laid out in Government securities until a proper Dissenting

* MS. *Account*, by Ri. Evans.

Minister should be chosen to the satisfaction of the congregation ; from which time the interest of the said £300 was to be paid to, and for the use of such the Minister of the said congregation for the time being. And whereas I have laid out the sum of £300 in the purchase of £400 3 per cent reduced Bank Annuities, and I have since paid the dividends thereof for the purpose of repairing the said Meeting House. Now my Will is, and I do hereby direct, that the said sum of £400 three per cent. reduced Bank Annuities be given to MARTIN BARR of the city of Worcester, China Manufacturer, the Treasurer of the aforesaid Society of Protestant Dissenters, THOMAS GILLAM, of Worcester, Mercer, JOSEPH FLIGHT, of Westminster, China Manufacturer, and ROBERT GILLAM, of Worcester, gentleman, their heirs and assigns ; upon trust to apply the same to the purposes aforesaid as far as my power extends under the said Will. Signed THOS URWICK, April 28, 1806. Proved 20th April, 1807." The probate is in the Will's Department, Somerset House. Entry in Cash book of Angel Street Church :—" 1814, Dec. 26, paid Mr. Joseph Flight, expenses £12 5s. 2d., of proving Rev. Mr. Urwick's Will."

In the later years of Mr. Osborn's ministry his boarding-school declined, and the congregation dwindled, owing in part to the failure of his health. He died at the parsonage house adjoining the chapel on Nov. 10, 1812, aged 54 years, and was interred in the burial ground adjoining the chapel, leaving behind him a widow, one son, and four daughters. In proof of the esteem entertained for him and his family, a sum was raised equal to the purchase of £40 annuity for his widow.*

* MS. by Mr. RICHARD EVANS ; *see also* NOAKE, *Worcester Sects*, p. 129.

On Nov. 23, 1812, the Rev. Dr. WILLIAMS, of Rotherham, presided, and gave an impressive address to the church, and Messrs. Barr, Ri. Evans, and Gillam were chosen as a Committee for procuring supplies. About this time, 1813, a letter was addressed to the church and congregation by a large number of ministers to the effect that " from a firm belief that the change recently adopted in the treasurership of your society is calulated to secure to you many important advantages, we beg leave to recommend it to your undivided and universal support. Two respectable members of your church have been regularly and jointly elected to the office, and to aid and encourage them in its discharge is, as we confidently believe, essential to the welfare of your congregation.

Signed by Revs.

WILLIAM THORP, Bristol.
THOMAS RAFFLES, Liverpool.
J. BERRY, Birmingham.
WILLIAM JAY, Bath.
JOHN HAMMOND, Handsworth.
JAMES ANGEAR, Hales Owen.
JOHN RICHARDS, Stourbridge.
JOHN HUDSON, West Bromwich.
J. BURDER, Stroud.
JOHN MANN, Morton-in-Marsh.
PETER EDWARDS, Wem.
JOHN WHITRIDGE, Oswestry.

SAMUEL LOWELL, Bristol.
J. BREWER, Birmingham.
J. A. JAMES, Birmingham.
ROBERT BOLTON, Glastonbury.
THOS. SCALES, Wolverhampton.
THOS. HELMORE, Kidderminster.
JAMES DAWSON, Dudley.
JAMES COOPER, West Bromwich.
WILLIAM BISHOP, Gloucester.
SAMUEL BARBER, Bridgenorth.
JOHN THOMAS, Cam.
JOHN LEWIS, Wooton-under-Edge.

Oct. 1, 1813, Jonathan Knott, Printer, Birmingham."

11.—The Rev. DANIEL FLEMING.

1814-1815.

10 May 1814, it was resolved at a Church Meeting that the Rev. Daniel Fleming, of Cork, be invited to take the pastorate at a salary of £200 per annum and the house. This invitation he accepted; but on March 3, 1815, he resigned. "We were ill prepared," writes Mr. Ri. Evans, "to meet the expenses attendant upon a minister's removal at so early a period after his settlement, especially with that liberality which became a Christian society towards one who had faithfully preached the Gospel to us. However, this was accomplished; and we were again as sheep without a shepherd, and, from Midsummer 1815 to Midsummer 1819, again dependent upon occasional supplies. During this period our views were directed to several ministers whom we thought qualified to fill the office; of these were Joseph Gilbert of Rotherham, Arthur Tidman of Salisbury, and Mr. Riley of Leicester. There was a considerable majority in favour of the last-named minister; but viewing unanimity of so great importance, the majority cheerfully bowed to the minority, and this act of prudence tended much to unite us together. From that time there has been as much unanimity existing in the church as we have a right to expect in this imperfect state."

12.—The Rev. Robert Vaughan.

1819-1825.

The Angel Street Church was next directed to the Rev. Robert Vaughan, then a student under the tuition of the Rev. William Thorpe of Bristol. He was of Welsh parentage, born in England 1795. He accepted the unanimous call in April 1819, and £500 were expended on the improvement of the chapel. Mr. Vaughan was ordained July 4, when the Revs. William Thorpe, S. Lowell of Bristol, Wm. Jay of Bath, John Angell James of Birmingham, took part in the service. Mr. Vaughan's ministry was highly acceptable; the congregation increased, and many were added to the church. In March 1825, he accepted a call from the church at Kensington. Here he remained twenty years. For a time he was Professor of Modern History in the University of London. In 1843 he became Principal and Tutor in Dogmatics at the Lancashire Independent College, a situation which he retained till 1857. He then accepted a call to a church in Uxbridge, but soon retired to St. John's Wood, and died at Torquay, June 15, 1868, aged 73 years. He was for twenty years editor of the *British Quarterly Review*, long since defunct; also the author of a *Life of John Wyclif*, the *Modern Pulpit*,

THE REV. ROBERT VAUGHAN, D.D.

Minister of Angel Street Church, 1819—1825.

Memoir of Stuart Dynasty, Revolutions in English History.*

II—The Rev. GEORGE REDFORD, M.A., D.D.

1826-1856.

July 9, 1825.—"It was unanimously agreed to invite the Rev. George Redford of Uxbridge to become our Pastor, offering him a sum of £300 per annum as requisite to support his numerous family. The Letter was signed by Robert Gillam and Richard Evans. On Oct. 18, the Rev. George Redford sent his reply accepting the invitation," and he continued Pastor for thirty years. He was the only son of the Rev. Alexander Redford, a Scotch Presbyterian, who, coming to England, became an Independent and was for more than half-a-century minister at Windsor. GEORGE REDFORD, having graduated at Glasgow, became pastor of the church at Uxbridge, where his preaching attracted much attention. "Mr. Redford," writes Richard Evans, "accepted our call, and commenced his stated labours in Midsummer, 1826. It had always been our anxious wish to obtain, if possible, a pastor for the church at Angel Street qualified from his experience and talent to take the lead in the county, and by his counsel and influence 'to break up the fallow

* *Congregational Year Book*, 1869. His only son, ROBERT ALFRED VAUGHAN was born and baptised at Worcester, 1823, graduated B.A. in Classics at London University, studied divinity at Lancashire Independent College, was assistant to Wm. Jay at Bath two years, pastor of Ebenezer Chapel, Birmingham, resigned in 1855; died Oct. 6, 1857. He wrote *Hours with the Mystics*, a much valued work. See *Congregational Year Book*, 1859.

ground and build up the old waste places.' This was the
strongest argument I could press upon him to give Worcester his most serious consideration. On this point I am
justified in saying that his efforts have been highly blessed
by God. There are few of the churches in the county and
its vicinity that have not received advantages from his aid
and guidance. The churches at Hereford and Bromsgrove
will stand as monuments of his successful efforts." *

In January 1827, he was led into a controversy from
which, when it came to be generally known that he had
taken part in it, he derived great reputation. A public
challenge to point out any errors in doctrine or morals of
the Romish church was accepted by him, and led to a controversy in which he displayed extraordinary learning, and
rare argumentative capacity. For a time the letters of
"Horace Bentley," under which signature he wrote, were
ascribed to Dr. Hook, then Dean of Worcester. The controversy ended in the Papist publicly confessing himself
beaten by the sources of argument agreed upon, viz., the
Christian Fathers. It was in connection with this controversy
that the University of Glasgow conferred upon him the
honour of LL.D. ; and shortly after a similar honorary
degree of D.D. was conferred by the University of Phila-
delphia.

Dr. Redford was a great supporter of the Literary and
Scientific Institution then existing in Worcester ; he was

* MSS. of Mr. Richard Evans, 1840.

THE REV. GEORGE REDFORD, D.D., LL.D.
Minister of Angel Street Chapel 1825—1856.

among the earliest antagonists of church-rates and the
corn-laws, and was a frequent contributor to the magazines
and reviews.   He was chosen Chairman of the Congregational Union for 1834, and delivered a series of Lectures
upon *The Holy Scriptures Verified.**

On Feb. 28, 1828, Messrs. STEPHEN BURDEN and
ROBERT NEWMAN were chosen deacons of the church.   It
was agreed that no one be employed as a village preacher
or reader of sermons, until he receive the sanction of the
minister or church.   Mr. Henry Humphreys was appointed
to preach at Droitwich, Ombersley, and Upton Snodsbury,
and Messrs. Charles Martin and Winspere be requested to
read sermons and conduct devotional exercises at Upton
Snodsbury ; the Rev. Geo. Redford to select such sermons
as he thinks most proper to be read.   Messrs. R. Newman
and Ri. Evans were deputed to receive donations to defray
expenses attending village preaching.

April 17, 1829.—Good Friday, being the day appointed
by the Congregational Churches as a day of humiliation and
prayer, the church met at 6.30 a.m., at 10.30, at 2.30 ;
and in the evening they united with the Baptist Church in
Silver Street, and with the Wesleyans in a devotional
meeting in Pump Street Chapel, when the three ministers
GEORGE REDFORD, THOS. WATERS, and JOSHUA MARSDEN
engaged in prayer, and delivered each a short address.

* Noake, *Worcester Sects*, pp. 136, 137.

Dec. 30, 1830.—Mr. THOMAS HILL, engaged in the Sunday School, and teaching in the Villages, having offered himself as a candidate for missionary work, received the sanction and recommendation of the church to the Missionary Society. This is one instance to show how from the Angel Street Sunday School, Teachers have gone forth as ministers, missionaries, or evangelists, and in other departments of Christian service.

"Sept. 8, 1848, Church Meeting.—It was resolved unanimously, that since it has pleased Almighty God to remove by death our much valued Deacon, Mr. RICHARD EVANS, after honourably discharging the duties of that office for thirty-four years, we place on record this testimony of our deep sense of his valuable services, of our respect for his memory, and of our gratitude to the great Head of the church for having spared him so long, and made him so useful to this Christian Society." *

"Nov. 3, 1854.—After a statement of the labours of the home missionary at Ombersley, and of the opening of a chapel at Hallow, resolved that Mr. THOMAS ROWLEY HILL, having purchased, repaired, and fitted up a small chapel at Hallow, and having offered the free use of the same to the Sunday School Committee, the Church accepts, thanks Mr. Rowley Hill, and prays for a divine blessing on the work there."

* *Minutes of Church Meetings*, Angel Street Church.

Nov. 20, 1856.—Dr. REDFORD, having suffered severe indisposition for more than twelve months, and all reasonable hope of recovery having vanished, addressed an affectionate letter of resignation to the church recounting the history of more than thirty years of peaceful and almost uninterrupted labour. Upon his retirement the church voted him an Annuity of £100, and presented him with a sum of upwards of £1000. After his retirement he resided at Edgbaston, Birmingham, occasionally visiting Worcester. In March, 1860, he administered the ordinance of the Lord's Supper in Angel Street Chapel. On May 16 he had an apoplectic seizure, and breathed his last on May 20, 1860, in his 75th year. His remains were interred in the graveyard at the back of Angel Street Chapel; on which occasion the Rev. T. R. Barker, tutor of Spring Hill College, delivered an impressive address, and the Rev. Robert Vaughan, D.D., preached on the following Sunday.

For literary avocations, especially those naturally issuing out of his ministerial character or cognate thereunto, Dr. Redford possessed qualifications far beyond the common range of even highly educated persons. Few outside the old Universities were more accurately learned in the Hebrew and Greek tongues, or more profoundly skilled in Divinity and Theology. He possessed extraordinary powers of observation and comparison, a quick and clear perception, great command of language, a singular faculty of combination, and remarkable administrative talents. There was a calm dignity and self-possession in his bodily presence which, when he entered any company, at once impressed even strangers. A man thus diversely gifted, and a ripe student besides, could not but have been of the utmost service to any cause which he espoused, and we may fairly describe Dr. Redford as a great pillar and ornament of Nonconformity. His active and comprehensive mind was by no means confined within the limits of his pastoral charge. Whilst ever faithfully discharging this, any movement that a man in his profession could with propriety co-operate in, whether for advancing the social, the moral, or the religious welfare of those amongst whom his lot was cast, might always count upon receiving his support.

He was constant and earnest in pleading the cause of the Bible Society, of all Missionary schemes, of the Antislavery Society, and always ready to lend his aid in promoting objects of piety, charity, or benevolence. He was instant in season and out of season in all works which had for their aim to elevate the social condition of the citizen, to increase his comforts, to liberalise our institutions and promote good government, to spread sound moral and religious knowledge, the better inculcation of Christian doctrine, and the extension of the Redeemer's kingdom. As a preacher he was original, eloquent, and argumentative, always felicitous, and often pungent in illustration, never failing to interest, but always carrying his hearers along with him ; dexterous exceedingly in the practical application

The Rev. William Flavel Hurndall, M.A., Ph.D.

Minister of Angel Street Church, 1857—1860.

of his theme, and in making a discourse tell upon the audience to whom it was addressed, much resembling in this respect his friends the Rev. Dr. URWICK of Dublin, and the Rev. J. A. JAMES, of Birmingham, with whom he was intimately associated during his career in Worcester.*

14.—The Rev. WILLIAM FLAVEL HURNDALL, PH.D., M.A.

1857–1860.

W. F. Hurndall succeeded Dr. Redford, entering on the pastorate in October, 1857. In 1858 Messrs. THOMAS ROWLEY HILL, CHARLES MARTIN, DAVID EVERETT and RICHARD JORDAN were elected Deacons. It was determined to rebuild the chapel; Alderman Padmore, afterwards M.P. for Worcester, gave £1000, and other leading members £500 each. Speaking thirty years afterwards at the Bicentenary meeting in 1887, Dr. Hurndall said:—"I came to Worcester as a youth almost fresh from college with great fear and trembling as Dr. Redford's successor. From the members I received much kindness, especially from the quaint and kindly Mr. PADMORE. In the old chapel were two extraordinary pillars that extended from floor to roof,

---

* In the *Dictionary of National Biography* a full memoir of Dr. Redford's life and work is given. He was born in London, 1785, educated at Hoxton Academy, and in Glasgow College, where he graduated M.A. in 1811. His first pastorate was at Uxbridge, 1812, and while there he edited the *Congregational Magazine*, and compiled (with H. T. Riches) a history of Uxbridge. For a list of his works see *Dict. of National Biog.*

designated by some, Jachin and Boaz. New comers were
induced to take sittings behind these immense pillars, and,
complaining that they could not see the preacher, were told
'that faith cometh by hearing.' This did not settle their
minds, and it was resolved to substitute a more modern and
commodious BUILDING. In this we had valuable help from
the late JOSEPH WOOD, a man highly esteemed as a citizen
and a Christian. We had the largest from Mr. PADMORE
and four others who raised the first total of £3000. Mr.
WILLIAM JOSELAND was one of the most energetic collectors.
One day when he was calling upon a contributor, there was
in the room a very poor woman regarded as a pensioner of
the church. We generally called her 'Poor Mary.' Mr.
Joseland was going out of the room without asking her for
anything when she stopped him and said, 'You don't ask
me for anything.' He replied, 'No, we consider you to
be too poor to help in anything of this sort.' She said, 'I
have enough in the bank to pay for my funeral, and I am
quite sure my friends will not let me want, therefore put me
down for £2.' I remember seeing the list of subscribers.
Poor Mary was at the top with £2, and Mr. Padmore
£1000. *Angel Street* has many associations connected with
its name. May this chapel always make this to be an Angel
street, a Mahanaim, a *via sacra*, where there shall be visits
of angels, frequent and full of blessing."[*]

The new building, which cost £5800, was opened on May

* *The Bi-centenary Supplement*, p. 7.

THE REV. JOHN BARTLETT.

Minister of Angel Street Church, 1840—1870.

31, 1859. Sermons were preached in the morning by the
Rev. SAMUEL MARTIN, of Westminster, and in the evening
by the Rev. NEWMAN HALL, LL.B., son of Mr. Vine Hall,
formerly bookseller, of Worcester. T. ROWLEY HILL, then
Mayor of Worcester, presided at an Afternoon Meeting.
The collections amounted to £275. On Feb. 2, 1860, Dr.
Hurndall was obliged through ill health to resign the
pastorate.*

15.—The Rev. JOHN BARTLETT.

1860-1870.

John Bartlett commenced his ministry here on Sunday,
Aug. 19, 1860. He was born at Portsea, Dec. 26, 1828.
His education was for a time pursued under the Rev. W.
Arnot of Portsea, and afterwards as a student of New College,
London. In 1855 he became co-pastor with Dr. Bennett
at Falcon Square. Thence he came to Worcester. In 1870
he went to Park Church, Halifax ; and in 1875 to Castle
Gate, Nottingham. His health giving way, he removed to
Forest Hill, but had to retire altogether from active service
in 1886. Regarding ANGEL STREET, he writes, " I went to
a handsome new Chapel just opened and paid for. The
partially scattered congregation were gathered, and the

---

* Dr. Hurndall was born at Basingstoke, July 10, 1830. After leaving Worcester he
was Head Master at Mill Hill three years, and then kept a private school at Rickmansworth,
1864-1883. After a short ministry at Littlehampton, he retired to Scarborough, where he
died, Aug. 19, 1888.

K

larger chapel filled. Then followed years of steady, united, fruitful work, the people responding to every call with a vigorous activity and great liberality."

28 January, 1861.—The Draft of a Trust Deed of the New Chapel at *Ombersley* was presented and approved ; and Thomas Rowley Hill, Joseph Grainger, D. Everett, Richard Joseland, C. Martin, James Tomlins, Fredk. Kelly, E. Wall, Wm. Joseland, George Brecknell, and Joseph Brecknell were elected to be Trustees.

Sept. 2, 1860.—The Pastor informed the Church that the Chapel at *Fernhill Heath* had been opened under favourable circumstances, and a Sabbath School commenced there.

March 2, 1864.—Mr. JOSEPH GRAINGER presented a Report from the Home Mission Committee, stating that some land and a Cottage at *Pole Elm* had been purchased by him, and that he was willing to make over the property to the Church if they would undertake the responsibility of providing a Chapel and Schoolroom. On March 20th, it was resolved that the Church approves of the property being placed in trust, and that the Home Mission Committee be requested to proceed with building a chapel as soon as funds can be provided.

10 Oct., 1866.—The death of Mr. CHARLES MARTIN was reported. A sympathetic resolution was passed recording that Mr. Martin was the oldest church member, having joined the church, Dec. 29, 1815.

The Rev. Robert Vaughan Pryce, LL.B.

Minister of Angel Street Church 1871–1876.

31 Aug., 1870.—Rev. John Bartlett resigned the pastorate on account of Mrs. Bartlett's health. On Sept. 7 a resolution was passed, unanimously regretting Mrs. Bartlett's illness, recording that the resignation did not proceed from any want of cordiality between pastor and people, recounting the affectionate earnestness of Mr. Bartlett's ministry, and his great devotedness to the interests not only of the church, but of the whole county. He afterwards became pastor of a church at Nottingham, and continued there till 1886. He took part in Bi-centenary Celebration of 1887.

16.—The Rev. ROBERT VAUGHAN PRYCE, LL.B.

1871–1876.

Feb. 8, 1871.—The Rev. Vaughan Pryce accepted the pastorate of the church.

25 Feb. 1874.—Mr. George Edwards was appointed an evangelist (salary £70) to visit and preach in the villages under the direction of the Pastor.

July 3, 1872.—A room in the adjoining premises was rented and fitted up for the INFANTS' Class.

" 26 Feb. 1873.—Regarding the use of sacramental wine at the Lord's Supper it was carried unanimously that the use of unfermented wine in the village stations be sanctioned, and that the vestry be instructed to arrange a separate service in the adjoining chapel with unfermented wine for those who prefer it."

In a letter noticing a series of sermons delivered by Mr. Vaughan-Pryce upon special subjects, the late Mr. JOHN NOAKE, writing in January, 1873, said :—

These sermons would do credit to the pulpit of any Christian Church, and ought to be accepted and prized by all of every denomination who value zealous and highly skilled labour in the cause of religion. A course of Paley, Butler, and other first-class writers on the subjects indicated, is to be enjoyed only by those who have considerable time and abilities of no mean order at their disposal ; but Mr. Pryce's sermons have popularised the great Doctors in Divinity in a way peculiarly his own, being pregnant with the rich fruits of deep and extensive research, presented in a masterly and original manner.

Dec. 20, 1876.—The Rev. R. Vaughan Pryce announced that he had accepted a call from the church at Stamford Hill, that in so doing he was obeying the Will of God, that his relations to this Church and its officers were of the happiest kind. A resolution was passed unanimously regretting the resignation, expressing affectionate regard to Mr. Pryce, and rejoicing that the resignation was not occasioned by diminution of affectionate sympathy between pastor and people.

The Rev. ROBERT VAUGHAN PRYCE was born in Bristol,

THE REV. SEPTIMUS MARCH, B.A.
Minister of Angel Street Church since 1877.

Dec. 15, 1834. His mother was a sister of Dr. Robert Vaughan, and his father was for many years Librarian to the city, and a fellow of the Society of Antiquaries. R. V. Pryce was educated in Queen Elizabeth's Hospital, Bristol, and after some years in business, entered New College, and graduated in London, B.A. in 1859, LL.B. in 1860, M.A. in 1861. He was minister in Brighton from 1862–1871; in Worcester, 1871–1876; in London (Stamford Hill), 1877–1889, when he came to be Principal of New College, Hampstead.

17.—The Rev. Septimus March, B.A.

From 1877.

In July, 1877, Rev. Septimus March, pastor of Albion Street Chapel, Southampton, accepted the call of the church to the pastorate. A new house at Battenhall was built for the pastor in the following year. In June, 1880, Mr. Marsh was laid aside by serious illness.

Mr. Everett, leaving Worcester, resigned the deaconship; and the church passed a resolution recognising Mr. Everett's Sabbath services extending over 23 years. He died in 1884, having been 39 years a member. In 1881, Messrs. Townshend, William Joseland, and Henry Day were elected deacons.

Mr. FRANK JOSELAND was, in April, 1882, recommended for admission to Spring Hill College as a missionary student. In the same year the Pastor reported the formation of an Association of Worcester Free Churches, and it was agreed that this church join the Association. It was also resolved to celebrate the Bi-centenary of the open enrolment of this church under the pastoral care of THOMAS BADLAND in 1687, by an improvement in the Sunday school accommodation. In 1887, Messrs. W. TEMPLE BOURNE, THOMAS BRYCE, and W. E. TUCKER were elected deacons.

SEPTIMUS MARCH, son of Henry March, Congregational minister, was born at Newbury, Berks, in 1840. He was educated at a school at Taunton, afterwards designated "Independent College," and entered Cheshunt College in 1858. In 1860 he graduated B.A. in the London University. After five years study under Dr. Alliott first, and after him Dr. Reynolds, he undertook the pastorate of Albion Chapel, Southampton, when he was ordained, June 3, 1863; the Revs. Thomas Atkins and John Woodwark took part, and the Rev. Henry March, his father, gave the charge. During his pastorate here of fifteen years the membership of the church was doubled.* Coming to Worcester in 1877, he took great interest in the BI-CENTENARY CELEBRATION. The site, costing £2600, for the new Sunday School was given by Mr. T. ROWLEY HILL, who also contributed £1000 towards the building, which cost nearly five thousand pounds.

* While here he published *Memorials of Charles March, Commander, R.N.*, afterwards issued by the *Religious Tract Society*, under the title, *Life on the Deep*.

The foundation or memorial stone bears the following inscription :—

THIS MEMORIAL STONE
OF NEW SUNDAY SCHOOL BUILDINGS
ERECTED IN CONNECTION WITH
THE BI-CENTENARY OF THE
FOUNDING IN 1687 OF THE
CONGREGATIONAL CHURCH, WORCESTER,
WAS LAID BY
MR. T. ROWLEY HILL, J.P., D.L.,
MAY 1, 1888.

The building consists of a central hall with gallery on three sides, and 22 class-rooms opening to the area and gallery, so that in very few minutes the entire school can be summoned from several class-rooms for united service. The young men's and young women's classes in the new building increased at once and rapidly, and are a great power for good, many being Church members. They have *Mutual Improvement* and *Christian Endeavour* Societies. It is confidently hoped that these beautiful and commodious rooms will be the home of the school and the nursery of the church for many generations.* Mr. March informs me that the membership of the church has increased from 238 in January, 1878, to 426 in the beginning of 1896. In the *Bi-centenary Supplement* of the Angel Street Church, published in 1887, we find the following :—" Broadness of mind and intellectual sincerity are among the best traditions of

* Statement of Mr. WALTER PRICE, one of the Superintendents of the Sunday School at Angel Street, April 21, 1896.

the past in Angel Street. Those qualities are happily well represented in the present minister. Under Mr. March's direction the organisation of Angel Street Chapel has been efficiently maintained in every branch." Owing to ill-health the church granted him a six months furlough in 1895, during which the services were conducted by Mr. Donald MacDonald, student of New College, who still remains as assistant to Mr. March.

Thomas Rowley Hill, Esq., J.P.

Our history would be obviously incomplete without a brief notice of the senior Deacon of the Worcester Congregational Church.

Thomas Rowley Hill, son of William and Elizabeth Hill, was born at Stourport in this county on March 1, 1816. His parents were active and consistent Nonconformists. When John Wesley came to Stourport, among those who were early moved by his teaching were Mr. Hill and Mr. Rowley who, with a few other residents in that town stood by him, and resolutely held their ground against the crowds that were ready to handle the preacher roughly. The son of this Mr. Hill was William Hill, F.R.A.S., who married a daughter of Mr. Rowley, who had stood beside his father in resisting the mob and protecting Wesley. Thomas

ROWLEY HILL is their son. In 1822 the family removed to
Worcester. His mother was a member of the Wesleyan
church ; his father became member and afterwards a deacon
of the Congregational church in Angel Street. Having
received his early education, he was sent to London to study
at University College. As a member of the firm of Hill,
Evans and Company, he engaged in business. In 1833,
he became a member of the Angel Street Church, and on
June 26, 1838, he married the daughter of Mr. Richard
Evans, deacon and trustee of this church, but she died
within a year of her marriage, on May 5, 1839. In 1842,
July 26, he married the daughter of the late EDWARD
EVANS, J.P., of Worcester, a prominent and highly respected
burgess, and also a member of the Congregational Church.
In 1857, he was elected deacon, and in the following year
(1858), he filled the office of Mayor of Worcester. He was
chosen Justice of the Peace for the city in 1860, and for the
county in 1865. He was made High Sheriff of the county
in 1870. He was elected Member of Parliament for Worcester in 1874, and was in the House of Commons twelve
sessions, till 1885. During this period he was a consistent
supporter of Mr. Gladstone and the Liberal Party. His
vote was always given on questions of importance to Dissenters. His constituents did him the honour of placing
his portrait, painted by Frank Holl, in the Worcester Guildhall.*

* See *Celebrities of the Day,* Nov. 1881, pp. 127-133.

As a deacon and trustee of the Congregational Church
the kindness of his heart and the liberality of his hand have
found their fullest expression.   The record of chapel and
schools bears abundant witness to his wisdom and strong
common sense in guiding, and his promptness in responding
to every proposal for the advancement of the Redeemer's
Kingdom ; and his help and sympathy have not been confined to the Congregational Church, but have gone forth to
sister churches and to beneficent societies at home and
abroad.   It is at his suggestion and in compliance with his
request that this work has been compiled.

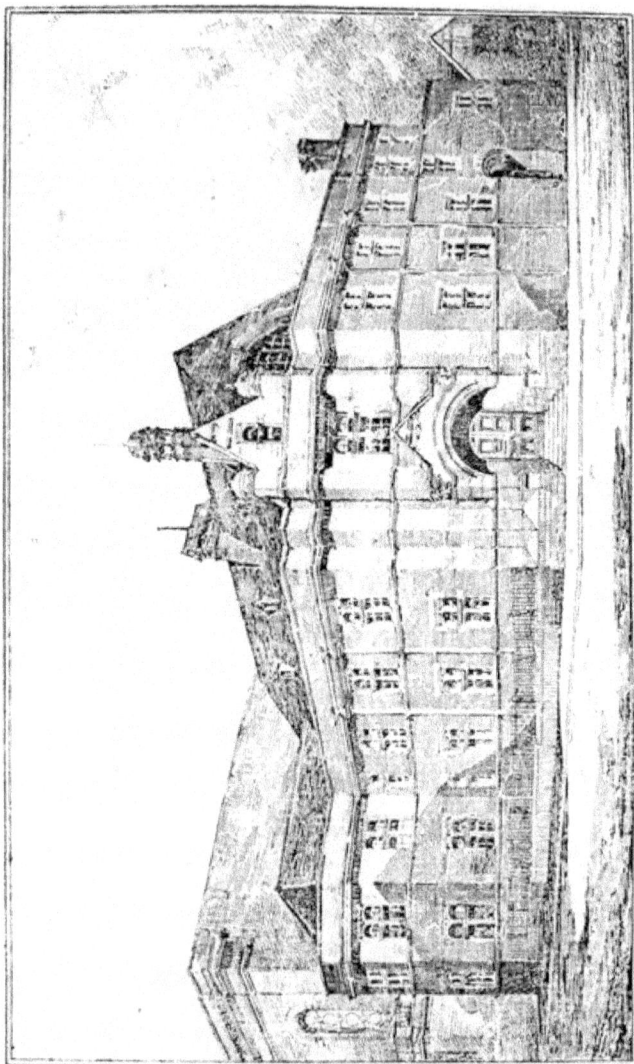

New Sunday Schools, Congregational Church, Angel Street, Worcester.

VII.

The Angel Street Sunday Schools, 1797 to 1897.

[By Mr. Walter Price, one of the Superintendents.]

URING the first decade from the commencement of Sunday schools by Robert Raikes in Gloucester, in 1780, their growth was small. Here and there some large hearted friend of children caught the idea, and made efforts to follow the example ; but generally the method was so novel, and, to the majority of people, so impractical, that little was done. Gradually, however, the thing grew, and during the second decade, 1790 to 1800, considerable advance was made.

The church in Angel Street was early in the field, and there can be little doubt that the first Sunday school in

the city of Worcester was that established in 1797 by the
Rev. G. OSBORN, the then pastor.   Mr. Osborn was a man
of large benevolence and tender spiritual sympathy for the
young.   He fairly doted on his Sunday school, fostering it
with a tender wisdom which could not fail to secure success.
The first school, which was exclusively for boys, dates 1797 ;
a second for girls was commenced in 1798—each having 50
to 60 scholars, so that they are now rapidly approaching
their centenary.   It is curious at this distance of time to
note that Mr. Osborn should have found it necessary in a
sermon preached at Angel Street, November 9, 1800, to
defend and vindicate the movement from the astounding
proposition that the schools were " Seminaries of Atheism."
In spite, however, of misunderstanding and opposition progress was marked, and we find early reference made to the
establishment of schools at Birdport, Countess of Huntingdon's, and at Pump Street Wesleyan Chapels.

Mr. Osborn passed to his eternal rest on Tuesday,
November 10, 1812.   His singularly beautiful character and
devotion to his cherished work has borne abundant fruit ;
and to this day some of his descendants are actively engaged
in the Sunday school.

It it interesting to note that at the time of Mr. Osborn's
death the Sunday school work was progressing in England
and Wales by leaps and bounds.   In 1813 a great meeting
of the " Society for the support and encouragement of

Sunday Schools" was held in London under the presidency of Mr. W. H. HOARE, at which it was stated that the Society had distributed 357,385 spelling books, 75,179 Testaments, 8,078 Bibles to 3,935 schools containing 324,000 children. In this year also we read that Mr. CHARLES of Bala gave an encouraging account of the work in Wales which led to the formation of the Bible Society.

To trace the history of the Sunday School is like following the course of a river, which though small in its beginning, gradually deepens and widens as it flows, beautifying the landscape and fertilizing the adjacent land. At no period since their establishment have the Sunday schools at Angel Street failed to occupy an important position in the organizations of the Church. A comparison of figures at different periods will serve to illustrate this. Thus, in 1870 the number of scholars, all included, was 392; in 1890, little more than a year after the opening of the new school buildings there were 520, at about which number they have since stood; as many as can be conveniently taught.

But numerical increase, although important in itself, fails entirely to gauge the nature and extent of the spiritual influences which have flown from this effort. Much of the best life of the Church has been nurtured here. Talents sanctified and employed in this sphere of Christian service, have been used by the Master for blessed results. It would be simply impossible to estimate the number of those who during the 100 years now ending have passed from the schools to the heavenly home, or to say how far-reaching have been the spiritual results. Ministers and missionaries, preachers and evangelists, workers in every department of Christian service have gone forth, and are still going forth from these schools. It may be mentioned also that two former superintendents have been called by the people to represent the city in Parliament, and nearly every municipal office has been filled repeatedly by those who have been active Sunday school teachers and officers.

Any account of Angel Street Sunday schools which left out of view the accommodation which has been provided for teachers and scholars would be incomplete. In this respect the Church has nobly done her part, coming forward from time to time to supply the growing needs of the schools.

In the bi-centenary year of the founding of the church, 1887, the crowning effort was made. It was then that a splendid site adjacent to the chapel was acquired by Mr. T. Rowley Hill, and generously conveyed to the Building Committee together with a cheque for £1000 as the starting of a building fund.

Much enthusiasm was awakened, and on May 1, 1888, the foundation or memorial stone of the present beautiful and convenient school buildings was laid. The inscription which is engraved upon the stone has already been given. The approximate cost of the Buildings and Site was £7,000.

They consist of a large hall, surrounded on two sides and one end, by a gallery. There are 22 class-rooms, ranged around, opening to the area and gallery floor, so that in a very few minutes the whole of the school can be called together from their separate rooms for united service. This arrangement is most convenient, greatly promoting the comfort of all engaged in the work.

It is confidently hoped that these beautiful and commodious rooms will be the home of the school for many generations. The senior department of the school was the one in which the benefit arising from enlarged and improved premises was most apparent. The young men's and young women's classes increased at once and rapidly, and are to-day a great power for good, a large proportion of the members are members of the church, and many engaged in Christian work in home mission and village services. Nor does the work end on Sunday; the young men hold a weekly meeting for mutual improvement and debate, whilst the Young People's Society of Christian Endeavour invites both sexes to a weekly meeting for praise and prayer, and study of God's Word.

The Sunday School has lately been exposed to some rather searching criticism from professional and other chairs; and some are inclined to think scant justice is being done to the devoted teachers who at much self sacrifice are giving themselves to the work. That the future of the Sunday

School will be one of increased efficiency and greater
spiritual power, none who note the signs of the times, can
doubt.   Meanwhile, let us give praise to God for all that
has been wrought.   If the good man, Mr. Osborn, who
founded the schools at Angel Street one hundred years ago
could see the work to-day, might he not say, "What hath
God wrought," and if he looked out on the wider sphere of
England and the world might he not add, "Surely the
little one has become a thousand, the small one a nation."

VIII.

The Baptists in Worcester.

HAPPILY the Rev. William Belsher, pastor of the Baptist Church, Silver Street, in 1796, records in the Church Book, that he had before him an old MS. volume belonging to the Baptists in Worcester, bearing this title :—

"A Book of the records of the Church of Christ in Worcester, made in the 11th month of the year 1658, by THOMAS FECKNAM ; consisting of Believers baptised with water in the name of the Lord Jesus." The next leaf begins, "The names of the members of the church, both brethren and sisters." The first name is Thomas Fecknam, and with him seventeen men and twenty-one women ; in all thirty-nine members. It does not appear, continues Mr. Belsher, "that Mr. Fecknam wrote any more in the book

L

than the title page, the names of the members already noted, and some queries resolved at Alcester by the messengers of the Associated churches, met there the 12th and 13th days of the 2nd month, 1659, at which time the church at Worcester tendered with them by mutual consent. Two of these queries were from Worcester. It is probable that Mr. Fecknam was the minister. The name of one of the women members is Sarah Fecknam. As he wrote no more in the book, probably persecution drove him away and scattered his flock."

From the Townsend MSS. it appears that on March 28, 1663, two of the Worcestershire Justices, Messrs. Townsend and G. Symonds, released out of the castle goal at Worcester, fourteen Baptists and many Quakers. In the Worcester county records the gaoler's list of prisoners in 1667 included Thomas Fecknam, said to be a leader of *the Quakers.* No doubt this was the Baptist minister.[*]

We have already given (p. 68) Calamy's account of the imprisonment of Robert Humphrys of Claines, and Mr. Pardoe imprisoned at Worcester in 1664.

"The next page" says Mr. Belsher, "of the Worcester records runs thus :—*The Restitution of the Church of Christ in Worcester the 10th of the 12th month 1666 to her communion and fellowship with Him.* On this restitution their names are put down, being but eleven men members,

---

[*] *Worcester Sects,* by John Noake, pp. 156, 162, *sqq.*

and ten women ; in all twenty-one. The first name is JOHN
EDWARDS, who afterwards lived at Leominster. There, it
is noted, he was brought very early to Christ, and was a
great encourager of believers when he lived in Worcester.
ELISHA HATHAWAY is the second person named. He began
to preach in this church about 1674, or possibly sooner, as
he was then aged about forty. He was very useful through
many years of persecution."

In the Lambeth MSS. is the following list of Anabaptist
conventicles in or about Worcestershire in 1669.

Parish.	Sect.	Number.	Quality.	Heads and Teachers.
St. Nicholas in Worcester, in the house of Mr. JOHN EDWARDS.	Anabaptist.	About 40.	Of all sorts, and of good accompt.	Unknowne.
Bromsgrove and King's Norton.		Several conventicles, but very few considerable persons in them, and their preachers are sometimes Nonconformists, and in their absence other laymen. Their names unknown.		
Defford, at the house of WM. WESTMACOTE, who keeps a school.		20.	Mean.	
Kidmarley Dabilds.		60 or 80.		Mr. SMYTH, Mr. PRESTON, Mr. JOHN GILES
Lapworth, at the house of a poor widow, ROGERS.		About 6 or 8.	Poore people.	Mr. FAUX of Henley.

Parish.	*Sects.*	*Number.*	*Quality.*	*Heads and Teachers.*
Alcester, one in the house of RICHARD JENNINGS, the other in the house of Mr. FRANCIS BRIDGES, and Sir JOHN.	Anabaptist.	At least 100.		Several lay persons.

There went out of this town seven score and odd persons against the king to Worcester.

Alderminster	Noe conventicle, but many seditious persons inhabite in this parish.			
Kingtone, at the house of John and Barbara Butler.	Anabaptists and Quakers.			See the names on the Return.
Whichford ...	... Anabaptists and other sects.	20 or 30.		JAMES WILLMORE, THOS. WHATELY, one WORDEN, Nonconformist.
Birlingham...	Noe conventicle, but some factious persons, inhabitants. See Returns for their names.			
Inkberrow, at the house of the widow STANLEY.	Quakers.	Sometimes 300 or less.		
Feckenham, at the house of JOHN FOYNES.	Anabaptists.			
Dormston, at house of the JOHN POOLE.	Anabaptist.	20 or 30.	Meane persons.	

Parish.	Sects.	Number.	Quality.	Heads and Teachers.
Kington, at the house of SAMUEL ROPER.	Anabaptist.	20 or 30.	Meane.	THOS. FECKENHAM.
Kington, at the house of WILLIAM HAYNES.	Anabaptist.	20 or 30.	Poore.	THOS. FECKENHAM, a cobbler, EAGLESON, a clothier, HENRY HANSOME.
Pershore, three conventicles.	1 of Presbyterians.	40 or 50.		
	1 of Independents.	30 or 40.		
	1 of Quakers.	12 families.*		

Among the places and persons licensed for preaching under the Indulgence of Charles II., 1672, are the following :

"The house of THO. CHAPMAN at Whittington, Baptist, 25 July, 1672.

Licence to MANASSES KING, to be an Anabaptist teacher in the house of Thomas Chapman.

The house of JOHN LANGFORD of Kierwood in Worcestershire, Anabaptist.†

At a meeting held May 27, 1692, ELISHA HATHAWAY was nominated as pastor ; W. Randal and W. Charles, elders ; Matthew Handy and Richard Hampton, deacons. During Mr. Hathaway's absence in London, Mr. HOLDER

---

* Lambeth MSS. 639 fol., 272 *sq*.
† R. O. Domestic, Interregnum, 3Sa.

preached at Worcester. By the the hand of JOHN WILLIS of Alcester and JOSEPH PRICE of Tewkesbury, brother Hathaway was ordained pastor. Mr. Pardoe who had been seven years in prison in Worcester was also in Hereford gaol four years. He died in Worcester 1692, leaving a sweet savour of Christ. Elisha Hathaway was pastor of the Baptist congregation in Worcester nearly forty years, and died in 1714, aged upwards of eighty years. The meeting house in Silver Street was built in his time and he was buried in it. The inscription on his grave run thus : " Here lieth the body of Mr. Elisha Hathaway, Gospel minister, teacher, and pastor of the congregation forty years ; having finished his work, by the Will of God he fell asleep in Jesus, 17 September, 1714, aged 81." *

Hathaway was succeeded by ISAAC POYNTING, who was minister some time at Frome in Somerset, but in 1715 removed to Worcester, where he died, May 5, 1740, aged 63 years, having been 25 years pastor. He was buried in the meeting house yard. He left a son in the ministry who succeeded him.

JOHN POYNTING, M.A., son of Isaac, was born at Worcester, October, 1719, and educated at Bristol under Messrs. Foskett and Evans. After some years of probation in the ministry at Worcester, he succeeded his father as pastor. He was reckoned a good scholar and rather a recluse. In

---

* William Belsher's account given by Mr. Noake in *Worcester Sects*, pp. 164-167.

1774 the College of Providence in Rhode Island gave him
the degree of M.A. His income was so small that he was
obliged to keep a boarding school. He died October 6, 1791,
aged 72 years. He was never maried. The Rev. Lawrence
Butterworth of Evesham gave an address at his grave and
preached the funeral sermon on Isaiah iii. 10, 11. Mr.
Poynting left upwards of £1200, of which he devised £200
to the particular Baptist fund in London for poor ministers,
£100 to the Widows' fund, and £200 to the Academy at
Bristol where he received his education. His only publica-
tion was a sermon preached before the Midland Association
at Bromsgrove, in 1768, on Psalm cxxxii. 16.*

After the death of John Poynting there was no pastor
from 1791 till the settlement of WILLIAM BELSHER, December 7, 1796. The chapel in Silver Street was rebuilt.
During the rebuilding the congregation met in Angel "Row"
or "Lane" Chapel, the use of which was given by the
Independents. Silver Street Chapel was re-opened July 27,
1797.

Mr. Belsher kept a boarding school for many years. He
usually had from thirty to forty boarders, and lived in the Red
House on Rainbow Hill, which commands a fine view of
the city. Among his pupils, 1807-8, was the present writer's
father, William Urwick from Shrewsbury (afterwards of
Dublin), regarding whom when a schoolboy Mr. Belsher

* Wilson's *Biog. Collections*, Dr. Williams's Lib.

writes: "If all my pupils were like William Urwick, teaching would be delightful work ; he receives instruction with so much meekness and gratitude (which is not common to youth) that we cannot but love him."*

William Belsher resigned the pastorate, from illness, on October 25, 1817. At that time the number of members was 112 ; and up to that time there had been only four successive pastors of the church for 143 years.

Henry Page, A.M., accepted the church's invitation to the pastorate, November 21, 1817. He was then in his thirty-seventh year. He had been about fifteen years in Bristol. He was pastor at Silver Street ten years, and died at Boulogne in 1833. The number of members was 150 at the time of his resignation.

Thomas Waters, who came from Pershore, succeeded Mr. Page on November 10, 1827, and resigned, from illness, August 31, 1838. He died two months afterwards. The number of members was then 199. During his ministry, namely in 1829, the chapel was considerably enlarged, a piece of ground adjoining having been purchased for the purpose at a cost of £275. The celebrated Robert Hall

* *Life and Letters of W. Urwick, D.D.,* p. 4. It may here be added that Mr. Richard Evans, so long an active officer of the Angel Street Church, had been apprentice in Shrewsbury to William Urwick's father, afterwards deceased, and acted with all the kindness of a guardian to the boy, inviting him to spend his holidays at his house, and shewing him attention in various ways. William Urwick was grand nephew of Thomas Urwick, minister of Angel Street Chapel. He preached in Worcester for three sabbaths in August, 1815, and for the Irish Evangelical Society in 1825.

of Bristol, and formerly of Leicester, preached at the re-opening from 2 Tim. iii. 5. F. J. Leifchild of Bristol, also preached from Psalm cxlix. 2.

ENOCH WILLIAMS was the next pastor, May 1839 to January, 1841.

WILLIAM CROWE followed in May, 1841, and was pastor for sixteen years. He was a man of unbending principle and irreproachable life. He was first an Independent, and a missionary in Travancore, having been trained at the Gosport College. Mr. JOHN NOAKE names him as one of four good men, uniting in their advocacy of every good cause, and stimulating their fellow citizens to lend their aid. They were JOHN DAVIES (Church of England), Dr. REDFORD (Independent), WILLIAM CROWE (Baptist), and SAMUEL DARKE (Quaker).[*] The Rev. J. J. WAITE's system of choral psalmody was adopted by Mr. Crowe's congregation, and the service of song was admirable. Mr. Waite resided at Hereford, but visited Worcester, where, though

---

[*] JOHN DAVIES was rector of St. Clements from 1816 till 1858. SAMUEL DARKE died July 20, 1856, aged 86 years. When a youth he was imprisoned for refusing to serve or to pay when "drawn" for the Militia. He joined the Society of Friends on Feb. 29, 1793, and for sixty-three years was ever among the foremost in demonstrating the folly and wickedness of coercion in matters of religion, in promoting temperance, the circulation of the Scriptures, home missions, and in denouncing the slave trade, the corn laws, and capital punishment. His exertions in the anti-slavery cause were acknowledged in 1839, when his fellow citizens presented him with a timepiece bearing this inscription :—" To SAMUEL DARKE for thirteen years acting secretary to the Worcester Anti-Slavery Society, presented by his coadjutors as a testimonial of their esteem for his long, unremitting, gratuitous, and unobtrusive services, by which, more than by the individual efforts of any other fellow citizen, they believe the glorious triumph of negro freedom in the British Colonies to have been accelerated." NOAKE, *Worcester Sects,* pp. 288-292.

completely blind, he instructed large classes with great
success. Mr. Crowe resigned his ministry in 1857 after
sixteen years' labour.*

In January 1858 the Rev. H. E. Von Sturmer, M.A.,
succeeded to the pastorate. He was son of F. Sturmer,
rector of Heapham, Lincolnshire, educated at Merchant
Taylor's School, entered St. John's, Cambridge, and was
baptised by Baptist Noel in 1856. The number of members
in 1860 was 200. In 1863-4 a new Gothic chapel was
erected in Sansome Walk at a cost of £5000.

Mr. Sturmer's pastorate terminated in 1873. He was
followed by the Rev. T. G. Swindill who was here two
years, 1874-1876. The Rev. James Lewitt undertook the
pastorate in 1876. He was educated at the Midland College, and entered the ministry in 1844. He was pastor
here fifteen years till 1890, when he retired, and still
resided at Kempsey. His successor was the Rev. Forbes
Jackson, M.A. of Glasgow, where he studied as well as at
Bristol. His ministry began in 1891, and he was pastor
here five years. The Rev. J. Bell Johnston, M.A., of
Edinburgh University and Pres. Theol. Hall, came from
Galashiels, where he was minister from 1887, and under-
the pastorate of this church, July 26, 1896. The present
number of members is 405.

* *Worcester Sects*, by J. Noake, pp. 173-178.

IX.

The Countess of Huntingdon's Chapel,
Birdport Street, Worcester.

EORGE WHITEFIELD preached his first sermon in Gloucester, his native city, June 26, 1736; but though frequently there and in many towns around, his memoir by Dr. Gillies makes no mention of any visits in Worcestershire until 1743, when he preached at Kidderminster and Bromsgrove. "At Kidderminster," he writes, "I was kindly received by Mr. Williams; many friends were at his house. I was greatly refreshed to find what a sweet savour of good RICHARD BAXTER's doctrine, works and discipline, remained to this day."*

* MEMOIR OF GEORGE WHITEFIELD, by John Gillies, D.D., p. 133. We have had a later testimony as to the tokens of Baxter's influence from the late Bishop CLAUGHTON, who was at Kidderminster 20 years. He told me that he could trace the teachings of Baxter in the habit of family worship still retained in many houses, as he visited down the street from house to house.

In 1748 Lady HUNTINGDON sent for Whitefield to preach at her house in London, and this he did usually twice a week to very brilliant audiences, among whom were Lords Chesterfield and Bolingbroke. This was the beginning of what grew into LADY HUNTINGDON'S CONNEXION. Whitefiield opened Lady Huntingdon's chapel in Tottenham Court Road in 1756; that at Bath in 1765. In 1768 he opened the chapel and college at TREVECCA, in the Parish of Talgarth, Brecknockshire, where HOWELL HARRIES laboured; the chapel at Tunbridge Wells in 1769.*

George Whitefield died 30 September, 1770, at Newbury Port, near Boston, New England, in the 56th year of his age. He graduated M.A. at Oxford, and was ordained by Bishop Benson when 22 years old, in 1736. Most of the early ministers of Lady Huntingdon's Connexion were episcopally ordained.

In 1757 an itinerant minister, Mr. Madan passed through Worcestershire, preaching in the parish churches; and Thomas Biddulph of Henwick Hill, opened his house for worship. In 1767, one of Lady Huntingdon's students, named ENGLISH, preached at Mr. Skinner's warehouse in the Town Ditch (Sansome Street). In 1769 Lady Huntingdon writes of Worcester, "Nearly 200 persons have been united in a religious society. The labours of Messrs. Glascott, Venn and others, have excited a disposition among

* *Memoir of Whitefield*, as before, p. 254, 256.

the inhabitants to attend to the things which belong to their peace." A chapel was built in Birdport and opened in 1773 by WALTER SHIRLEY and WILKS. Among the students who used to preach were Messrs. Wilks, Green, Hayes, English, Merror, Winkworth, Glascott, Newell, and Trench.* The following signatures of officiating ministers occur in the Register book of Baptisms at the Countess of Huntingdon's Chapel :—

Samuel Beaufoy, 1784 ;	John Child, 1788 ;
William Collins, 1788 ;	Lewis Jones ;
John Cureton ;	John Harris ;
John Dawson ;	J. Tissier, 1793 ;
Josiah Richards ;	T. Bennett, 1795 ;
J. Rust, 1796 ;	James Brotherton, 1798 ;
Robert Bradley, 1799 ;	John Griffith, 1800 ;
G. Evans ;	J. James, 1802 ;
John Chamberlain, 1804 ;	John Brown, 1804 ;
John Emblem ;	J. Whittingham, 1806.

Lady Huntingdon died in 1791,† and the chapel was bequeathed to trustees. In 1804 a more commodious

---

* JOHN NOAKE, *Worcester Sects*, p. 352. "In a note appended to W. H. Havergal's sermon on the death of John Davies, Rector of St. Clement's, it is recorded that the estimable father of an alderman in Worcester was hunted like a wild beast with all sorts of missiles along the High Street, because he had befriended a preacher of Lady Huntingdon's Connexion. The person alluded to was, I believe, the late Mr. JAMES ALLIES, a trustee of Birdport Chapel ; and he and his wife were often grossly insulted while going to and returning from that place of worship." *Ibid.* p. 355.

† Selina, Countess of Huntingdon was born 1707. She was daughter of Washington Shirley, second Earl Ferrers, born near Ashby-de-la-Zouch, Leicestershire, and in her twenty-first year married to Theophilus, ninth Earl of Huntingdon. Her husband died 1746, and from

chapel was opened by the Rev. JOHN BROWN, afterwards
Independent minister in Cheltenham. The Rev. JOHN
FINLAY was there about this time ; and in 1806 the Rev.
EDWARD LAKE, who became the resident pastor. His
ministry was so successful that in 1815 the building was
enlarged to seat 2000, and was opened by the celebrated
ROWLAND HILL. The following Trustees of the Chapel
sign the Register transfer in 1837 :—

> Thomas Barnes, Gentleman.
> William Causer, Glove manufacturer.
> Jno. Barker, Artist.
> William Lewis, Woollen Draper.
> Wm. Jones, Glove manufacturer.
> Josh. Wood, Builder.
> Wm. Collins, in America.

They intimate that the Rev. Edward Lake has kept the
Register books since 1810, and now holds them as minister,
May 2, 1837. He was minister 28 years, when he retired
and preached in a small chapel in Lowesmoor for the last
seven years of his life. He died in 1843, aged 64 years,

that time she spent her ample means in building chapels and supporting ministers in them as
her chaplains. They continued members of the Establishment till 1779, when a suit having
been instituted in the Consistory Court by the Rev. W. Sellon of St James's, Clerkenwell,
against two of her chaplains for carrying on Divine Service against his consent in his parish,
it was decided against her ; and she had no alternative save by becoming a Dissenter, to gain
the protection of the Toleration Act. Till her death in London, June 17, 1791, Lady Huntingdon exercised an active supervision of her chapels and chaplains, and maintained her
position by her genuine earnest piety and her generous liberality. Her chapels and college
were bequeathed to trustees ; and in 1792, the latter was removed to Cheshunt, Herts.
Encyc. Britannica, 9th edition, xii. 399.

after 33 years residence in Worcester. He was much attached to the Church Establishment. He was followed in the pastorate by the Rev. Mr. Hewlings, and in 1853 the Rev. T. Dodd became minister. He died at a great age very recently. The present minister, the Rev. E. J. Boon, came eleven years ago.

Schools were established by the Rev. John Harris in 1791, reorganized by the Rev. Robert Bradley who came in 1799. They have been extensively useful. Upwards of 300 children are instructed by 40 teachers.

Mr. Lake was succeeded at Lowesmoor Chapel by the Revs. E. Bayfield, Woods, Sanderson, Henry Wardley, during whose ministry the chapel was renovated and re-opened April 11, 1860. Mr. Joseph Wood (afterwards Mayor) was both architect and builder. Mr. Wardley was here about twenty years. He was followed by the Revs. John Webb (here about 18 months), and E. J. Bowen, who stayed only a few months. The next settled pastor, W. B. Birtt, remained twenty years. Mr. Enos Berry, a deacon of the Baptist church next officiated for ten years; and the Rev. W. Williams (a Cheshunt student), preached here for two years. There is no pastor at present.

APPENDIX.

I.

Walker's Sequestered Clergy.

NAMES of those sequestered in Worcestershire, 1643. Out of 252 parishes there were, according to Walker, only 39 sequestrations in this county; and even of these, several are mentioned in a vague, doubtful, fragmentary manner. Walker's spelling of names both of places and persons is retained.

Worcester, JOHN PRIDEAUX, D.D., Bp., 1641. He was plundered and forced to sell his library for bread for his family. "I have eaten," he said, "a great library of excellent books." He died in the house of his son-in-law, Dr. Henry Sutton, at Bredon in Worcestershire.

CHRISTOPHER POTTER, dean, once a zealous Puritan, and lecturer at Abingdon. Died March 3, 1645-6.

Richard Holdsworth, dean, born 1590; one of the Assembly of Divines in 1643. Charles I. made him Dean of Worcester, while Holdsworth waited on him at Hampton Court. Died, aged 58, in 1648.

EDWARD THORNBOROUH, archdeacon, 1629, son of the old bishop. Died 1645.

WILLIAM HODGES, archdeacon, May 30, 1645, Rector of Ripple in Worcestershire, allowed to keep his living. [Not sequestered.] Died 1676.

GILES THORNBOROUGH, nephew of the bishop, Vicar of Crawley and Wolverley, canon, 1629. [Not sequestered.] Died 1663.

FRANCIS CHARLES, canon, and Rector of Salwarp.

Giles Wooley, ejected from Salwarp in 1662.

Wm. Westmacott, said to come in after Dr. Charles and ejected from Cropthorn in 1662.

Anthony Tyringham, canon.

Nath. Tomkins, canon, son of Thos. Tomkins, an eminent and learned musician, Rector of Broadway. Died 1681.

NATH. GILES. Not mentioned by Nash.

WILLIAM SMITH, canon, Rector of Tredington. Died 1658.

HENRY WRIGHT, canon. Stephen Boughton, canon.

Thomas Lawrence, canon. Herbert Crofts, canon.

Robert White, canon.

Harvington, Thomas Archbold, died in London; his curate, W. Bridges, succeeded, and died 1654.

Lindridge, George Benson, seized by Court of Worcester, 1645, died 1647 at Rock, was succeeded by one G. [John Gyles, pastor of Lindridge, died 1661. Nash II. 99.]

Wolverley, Bowton.

Doverdale, Edwin Brace. [Not sequestered.]

Hampton Lovett, Cooper. [Not sequestered, see Survey.] Freestone succeeded, and was ejected in 1662.

Fridaysharp, Cooper.

Kidderminster, Dance (was restored), Ri. Baxter, ejected in 1662.

M

Blockley, Geo. Durant ; G. Collier succeeded and conformed.

Upton, Ri. Farley.

Hartleborough, ——— Thomas Wright got the living in 1655.

Church Lench, Holiead.

Alvechurch, Hollington, restored, Ri. Moore got it.

Estham, Francis Kelly.

Chadley Corbet, Lee or Leigh, restored, Thos. Baldwin succeeded.

Floyford, Benj. Masters.

White Lady Aston, John Moseley, Robert Brown succeded.

Ombersley, Pilkington.

Tredington, W. Smith (see above).

Stone, Spicer. [Not sequestered, see Survey.] Ri. Sergeant, his son-in-law followed.

Bredon, Sutton, restored, Beeston.

Old Swinford ——— Gervase Bryan followed.

Knightswick, Taylor, Matt. Bolton, 1654.

Dodenham, Thomas Warmestry, born in Worcester, dean after the Restoration.

Upton-on-Seven, W. Woodford, restored, died 1664 ; Benj. Baxter.

II.

Parliamentary Survey of 1650, touching Church Livings in Worcestershire.

AMBETH LIBRARY possesses among many valuable MSS. relating to the Commonwealth, the original RETURNS signed and sent to Parliament by the JURORS appointed for several Counties of England in the year 1650. The object of the Survey was "to make enquirie by sufficient able men upon oath, of the number of Parsonages, Vicarages presentative, and all other Ecclesiasticall liveings within the countey of Worcester with the values thereof with severall other thinges of us required as relation being had to the said commission more fully doth appeare." There is at Lambeth a very good *Index* to this Survey; the volume relating to Worcestershire is mainly No. 16. A complete summary of this Survey is in the British Museum Library.

Lambeth MSS. Survey of 1650, vol. 16.   Lansdown MSS., B.M. Lib., 459.

Parish.	Value.	Incumbent.
Broomsgrove Vicarage	...£70 0s. 0d.	John Hall, minister.
Chadwick Chapel (3 miles distant) ...	—	Without minister.
King Norton ...	40 0 0	Tho. Hall.
Mossly Chapel	4 13 4	Tho. Moore.
Whithall Chapel	5 0 0	Ri. Ward.

Parish.		Value.			Incumbent.
Droitwich, St. Peters...	...	40 marks			Thos. Garland.
Dodderhill	... ...	...£80	os.	od.	No minister, sequestered, still living, Will. Jones, sen.
St. Andrews, Droitwich		6	13	4	Rob. Norbury.
Mary Whitton, near D.		36	0	0	No minister, no church.
Nicholas ,,		26	0	0	No minister.
Rushocke		60	0	0	Henry Hunt.
Crowle... ...		50	0	0	Giles Thornburgh.
Sallwarpe ...	...	70	0	0	Rich. Woolley.
Hampton Lovett		50	0	0	Edw. Cooper.
Dovedale ...		25	0	0	Edwin Brace.
Elmly Lovett	...	70	0	0	Edw. Best.
Upton Warren and Cooksley...		—			Joseph Bennet.
Hadzor	...	35	0	0	William Jones.
Fleckenham	...{	4 20	10 0	0 0 }	John Mason.
Tardebigg ...		20	0	0	Edw. Cooke.
Boresley Chapel		—			No maintenance but what the inhabitants give him.
Old Swinford ...	...	110	0	0	Gervase Bryan by sequestration from Wm. Harewell.
Northfield ...	...	100	0	0	Timothy White.
Coston Chapel		20	0	0	Thos. Homan.
Churchill ...		40 marks			Rich. Penn.
Yardley... ...	...	50	0	0	James Archer.
Kington ...		49	6	8	Birch, by sequestration from Holden.
Frankley (Hales Owen, Salop)	Some small allowance from Sir Hen. Lyttleton				Henry Billingham.
Cradley...	...	—			Edw. Paston.
Warely Chapelry to Halsowen		15	0	0	Rob. Willmore.
Cudley ,,					
Pedmore ...	...	40	0	0	Tho. Malpas.

Parish.	Value.			Incumbent.
Dudley ...	...£50	os.	od.	
Stone ...	50	0	0	Spicer.
Church Lench ...	40	0	0	
Chaddisley	50	0	0	Sam. Lea.
Belbroughton	... 100	0	0	Rich. Tristram, presented by Roger Walden, yeoman.
Kidderminster ...	... 160	0	0	Ri. Baxter, by sequestration from Dance.
Mitton Chapel	... 10	0	0	Turner.
(Allowed by Rector of Kidderminster).				
Segesbarrow	73	0	0	Tim. Wharton, by sequestration from Turvey.
Cropthorne	70	0	0	Will. Westmacote.
Fladbury ...	60	0	0	Mr. Elliott, Ellis his curate.
Pinvin Chapelry	10	0	0	Pratt.
Bradley Chapelry				
Washbourne and Alston	20	0	0	Bernard Maunder.
Teddington ...				
Abburton ...	30	0	0	Edw. Kempster.
Broughton Hacket	26	0	0	Roger Saunders.
Rouselench	90	0	0	John Wall.
Elmly Castle	18	0	0	John Hancox.
Inkbarrow	... 100	0	0	Wm. Watson, sequestered from Whyte.
Bengeworth ...	18	0	0	No minister.
Evesham, All Saints ...	5	6	0	Geo. Hopkins.
St. Lawrence	—			Tho. Mathewes.
Dormeston ...	18	0	0	Tho. Taylor.
Comberton, Magna	26	13	4	Leonard Bagshaw [Baxter?]
Upton Snodsbury	14	0	0	William Shorte.
Burlingham ...	55	0	0	Ri. Conner.
Pirton ...	71	0	0	Will. Lovell.

Parish.	Value.			Incumbent.
Grafton Flyford	£100	0s.	0d.	John Dalbye.
Breedon ...	... 35	0	0	Rich. Beeston.
Norton Chapel	... 130	0	0	Jonathan Davis.
Culsdon Chapelry ...	... 35	0	0	Ambrose Joukes.
Eckington	... 20	0	0	No minister.
Whittington Chapelry to St. Peter's ...	... 3	19	0	Mr. Durman.
Kempsey ...	26	18	4	Tho. Bromwich.
White Lady Aston	50	0	0	Jasper Britten.
Churchhill	50	0	0	Tho. Barker.
Spetchley	34	0	0	Tho. Whitefoot.
Stoake Pryor ...	60	0	0	Ri. Dowley, by sequestration from Toy, fifths allowed.
Cotheridge	40	0	0	Theoph. Cooke (Sir Rowl. Buckley, £20).
Shellesley parva ...	26	8	4	Edw. Lane.
Clifton-upon-Teme ...	... 27	10	0	John Greene.
Keyer parva, Chapelry to Stoake blisse, Hereford ...	16	0	0	Edw. Russell.
Edvin Lench ...	... 14	0	0	Ri. Jay.
Keyer Magna ...	... 30	0	0	Hugh Thomas.
Persher Abbey...	30	0	0	John Cliffe.
Eastham ...	... 68	10	6	Edw. Benson.
Orlton Chapelry	—			Arthur Bolsey, curate to Mr. Benson.
Hanley Child Chapelry	16	0	0	John Philips, curate to Mr. Benson.
Horney Williams Chapelry	14	0	0	Benson and Philips.
Suckley... ...	... 95	0	0	Thos. Littleton.
Lulsey Chapelry ...	—			Wm. Doughty, curate to T. Littleton.
Alfriche Chapelry ...	0	16	0	Slade, curate to T. Littleton.

Parish.	Value.	Incumbent.
Stanford	... £40 0s .0d.	Tho. Stedman.
Bockleton	10 0 0	Tim. Harris.
Arley Kings	68 13 4	John Bayly.
Tenbury	30 0 0	Thos. Good, Clarke, as curate to Mr. Clent, Vicar of Rock, in Herefordshire.
Martley...	... 107 0 0	Thos. Clent.
Acton Beauchamp	40 0 0	George Fincher.
Shrawley ...	80 0 0	John Jorden.
Astley ...	... 160 0 0	Francis Marshall.
Stocton...	25 0 0	Tho. Roberts.
Hartlebury	... 250 0 0	Tho. Wright, by sequestra- tion from Smith; fifths allowed.
Bredicott	50 0 0	Will. Riccards.
Hanbury	180 0 0	John Vernon.
Oddingley	30 0 0	John Crumpe (presented by Sir Geo. Winter, Kt.)
Powicke	30 0 0	Eliezer Jackson.
Braunesford Chapelry	50 0 0	Ri. Berchett officiates here and at Lench.
St. Johns-in-Bradwardine	30 0 0	Dr. Wright.
Claines ...	30 0 0	Geo. Stinton.
Mathon...	22 0 0	No minister.
Ombersley	30 0 0	No minister.
Grimley... ...	3 0 0	John Shaw.
Hollow Chapelry	28 0 0	John Best.
Broadwas	40 marks	John Wall.
Seavernstoake...	... 160 0 0	Arthur Sallway.
Tibberton	16 0 0	Henry Wynde.
Hindley...	40 0 0	Rich. Woolley.

Parish.	Value.	Incumbent.
Huddington ...	... £17　os. od.	Wm. Warner (Sir G. Win-
Martin Hussingtree ...	... 28　o　o	Tho. Cooke.　　[ter £20).
Alvechurch ...	... 130　o　o	Rich. Moore.
Wichenford ...	60　o　o	Joseph Malden.
Woolverley	50　o　o	Laus Deo Malden.
Himbleton	20　o　o	Arthur Barton.
Warndon	50　o　o	Tho. Wyld.
Whitley parva, Chapelry to Holt	31　o　o	Geo. Davis, by sequestration from Pauling, fifths allowed.
Stoughton, Chapelry to Kempsey	18　o　o	Geo. Allen.
Holt ...	78　o　o	Isaac Charles, by sequestration from Panting, fifths.
Upton-on-Severn ...	200　o　o	Ben. Baxter, sequestered from Woodford, fifths allowed.
Barrowe　　£70 ...	18　o　o	Mr. Jackman.
Chaseley ...	12　o　o	Nath. Winsmore.
Gt. Malvern ...	8　o　o	John Ballard.
Bushley Chapelry ...	10　o　o	No minister.
Elderfield ...	30　o　o	Ri. Cole.
Longdon	20　o　o	Nich. Ferrett.
Queenhill Chapelry		
Holdfast Chapelry is decayed	50　o　o	Mr. Laight.
Staunton	70　o　o	Edm. Atwood.
Redmerley ...	... 100　o　o	No minister.
Birch Moorton...	55　o　o	Thos. Gilbert.
Castle Moorton	20 marks	Mr. Evans certified for want of a minister.
Welland ...	40　o　o	Mr. Evans.
Hanley Castle ...	30　o　o	James Warwick, by sequestration from Wheeler, fifths allowed.

Parish.	Value.			Incumbent.
Madderfield	...£55	os.	od.	Will. Elliot.
Ripple ...	... 200	0	0	Wm. Hodges.
Pendocke	... 60	0	0	Tho. Nanson.
Newland Chapelry 1 house	5	0	0	John Sayer.
Croom Dabitet	64	0	0	Nath. Alies, by order of the Committee.
Earl's Croome...	50	0	0	Rich. Bury.
Hill Croome ...	56	13	0	Mr. Evans.
Little Malvern...	—			Heywood.
Leigh ...	50	0	0	Bircher.
Old Barrow	40	0	0	Rob. Raynhow.
North and Middle Littleton ...	30	0	0	Henry Ballard.
South Littleton	25	17	4	Henry Ballard.
Alder Marsden	30	0	0	Wm. Dedicott, an aged man, unable to officiate ; Mr. Swan is his curate.
Bishampton	90	0	0	Mr. Reynolds.
Broadway	16	0	0	John Dolphin.
Throgmorton ...	6	0	0	Philip Rock.
Beoley	60	0	0	Late incumbent, W. Hatton, is sequestered. Fifths allowed.
Befford, chapel to St. Andrews, Parshore ...	12	0	0	Francis Shepherd.
Nanton Beachamp ...	70	0	0	Francis Robinson.
Parshore, St. Andrew	20	0	0	Thos. Bachler.
Wick *juxta* Parshore	8	0	0	Rob. Taylor.
Lenchwick, chapelry to Norton	12	10	0	Edw. Saunders.
Great and Little Hampton ...	4	0	0	No minister.
Harvington	100	0	0	Wm. Bridges, by sequestration from Archboulds, Fifths allowed.

Parish.	Value.			Incumbent.
Pippleton	£50	os.	od.	Cornelius Woodward.
Flivard Flavel	32	0	0	Giles Hartwell.
Pinvin, chapelry to Fladbury...	8	0	0	Ri. Print.
North Piddle ...	47	0	0	John Jones.
Wickhamford ...	20	0	0	Sam. Roe.
Offenham	8	17	0	Mr. Ambrose is vicar, Rich. Mansell officiates.
Strensham ...	50	0	0	Henry Miller.
Church Honeyborn	22	0	0	Will. Roberts.
Comberton Parva ...	22	0	0	Minister not named.
Badsey and Adlington	20	0	0	Ri. Cragg.
Bradferton	14	0	0	
Overbury	30	0	0	Philip Tinker.
Bricklehampton, chapelry to St. Andrew, Pershore	10	0	0	Ezekiel Coachman.
Icombe ...	40	0	0	R. Willett.
Evinlode	100	0	0	R. Nevill.
Cutson, chapelry to Breedon, 10 miles distant	24	0	0	Ambrose Joukes.
Treddington ...	403	0	0	Durham, by sequestration from Dr. Smyth.
Shipston, chapelry to Treddington ... ... / Tadminton	—			The minister has an allowance out of the Rectory.
Blockley	80	0	0	Giles Collyar, by sequestration from Durant.
Dartlesford	30	0	0	In strife between two ministers.
Cleeve Prior ...	40	0	0	Will. Wills.
Abbots Morton ...	60	0	0	Will. Tubbs.

Parish.	Value.	Incumbent.
CITY OF WORCESTER :—		
St. Swithen's	... £26 13s. 4d.	Rowland Crosby.
St. Clement's	6 0 0	Noe minister.
St. Peter's	6 0 0	Simon Moore.
St. Hellen's ...		
St. Martin's ...	70 0 0	Thos. Juice, by sequestration.
St. Michael in Bedwardine...	6 8 4	Mr. Simon Moore, by sequestration.
All Saints	5 10 0 a house.	Noe minister.
St. Nicholas...	8 10 0 a house.	Noe minister at present.
Shallesley Beauchamp	60 0 0	Charles Nott.
Mamble	20 0 0	Humphry Randall.
Bayton ...	24 0 0	Tho. Hart.
Rocke	120 0 0	Edw. Partington.
Hitchington, chapelry to Rocke	—	Mr. Berecroft is his curate.
Pensax, chapelry to Lindridge	10 0 0	Ri. Fincher.
Knighton, chapelry to Lindridge	26 3 4	Edw. Shaw.
Doddenham and Knightwicke, always united	60 0 0	Thos. Taylor.
Lindridge	... 100 0 0	John Giles.
Abberly	53 0 0	John Dedicott.
Bewdley	48 8 0	Henry Osland.
Ribsford	... 118 0 0	John Boraston.
Hagley ...	50 0 0	Barthol. Kettle. (Sir T. Littleton.)

LAMBETH AUGMENTATIONS.

Lambeth MSS., circ. 1656.*

Parish.	Minister.	Augmentation.		
Yardley...	Ja. Arthur.	...£40	os.	od.
Kempsey	Tho. Bromwich	... 24	14	4
Lindridge	Jo. Giles ...	... 30	0	0
Grimley...	Jo. Web	...⎰ 29	13	9
		⎱ 20	6	8
Cropthorne	Wm. Westmacott...	... 40	0	0
Hanly Castle ...	Ja. Warwick	50	0	0
Netherborough	Tho. Jackson	62	0	0
Throgmorton ...	Philip Rock.	30	0	0
Bewdley	Henry Osland ...	60	0	0
Crowle ...	Giles Thornburgh	... 40	0	0
Churchlench	Joseph Trebble	30	0	0
Standford	Tho. Stedman.	50	0	0
Worcester, St. Michaels ...	Symon Moore.	90	0	0
Worcester, All Saints and Nicholas	Ri. Fincher	49	15	3
Worcester, Martins ...	Tho. Juice ...	... 20	0	0
Welland ...	Tho. Evans	30	0	0
Selsey Beauchamp	Cha. Nott ...	36	13	4
Dudley	Jo. Taylor ...	26	0	0
Broadway	Joseph Watson	24	0	0
Evesham	Geo. Hopkins	65	0	0
Evesham ...	Thos. Mathewes ...	65	0	0
Evesham School ...	Jo. Japhcott	20	0	0
Worcester, Andrews	Joseph Baker	50	0	0
Wormley	Simon Potter	20	0	0

* 981 fol. 141, Worcester.

Parish.	Minister.	Augmentation.		
Icombe ...		£20	0s.	0d.
Gt. Malvern		20	0	0
Ombersley	Geo. Barraston	30	0	0
Kings Norton	Tho. Hall ...	20	0	0
Mitton Chappel in Kidder-minster ...	Tho. Soley	20	0	0
Bromsgrove ...	Jo. Spilsbury	50	0	0
Stoke Pryor	Ri. Dooley ...	40	0	0
Parshore	Jo. Wilmott	20	0	0
Mosley ...	Sam. Shaw	25	6	8
Eckington ...	Tim. Jordan	30	0	0
Withward Chapelry	Ri. Ward ...	13	6	8
Chasely... ...	W. Izard	10	0	0

LAMBETH MSS. AUGMENTATIONS, Vol. 982, fol. 226.

Parish.	Minister.	Aug.
Longdon, June 17, '58	Thos. White, 22 May last, 6 years	£200
Cropthorne, Mar. 11, '56 ..	Ri. Bulstrode	£105
Lindridge, Nov. 8, '51 ...	Edm. Gyles ...	£50
Lenchwick, Dec. 2, 1658	James Hawley	£150

ADMISSIONS.

LAMBETH MSS. AUGMENTATIONS, Vol. 999, anno 1658.

69. Oddingley. Edw. Phillips, upon Presentation from the Lord Protector, and Certificates from Ri. Vernon, Tho. Francis, Tho. Garland, Rob. Norbury of Droytwich, Ri. Wolley, Jo. Freesdon of Hampton Lovett.

163. Hindlipp. John Wolley, upon a Presentation from Thos. Solley, with Certificates from Thos. Wright, Thos. Juice, Jos. Baker,

Jo. Spilsbury of Broomsgrove, Tho. Francis, Tho. Garland, Rob. Norbury, Tho. Browning.

265. Lenchwiken. John Baker with Certificates from Thos. Mathew of Evesham, Joseph Trebell of Church Lench, Jo. Dolphin of Church Honiborne.

365. Abberley *als.* Abbotsley. Rob. Foulkes, upon a Presentation from his Highness Richard, Lord Protector, 25 Oct., 1658, with Certificates from Ma. Herbert, Jo. Aston, Robt. Goodwyn of Cleobury Mortimer, Wm. Whittell of Bromfield.

374. Flyford Flavel. Thomas Howes upon a Presentation from Anthony Sambatch, Esq., and Certificates from John Brian, Hen. Butler, Jo. Dawley, Tho. Dugard, Jo. Trap, Anth. Nodhall.

388. Great Whitley. Joseph Read upon a Presentation from Thos. Foley, Esq., and Certificates from Andrew Tristram of Bridgnorth, Tho. Baldwin, Jarvis Bryan, Jos. Baker, Ric. Sarjeant.

431. Treddington. William Durham, B.D., upon a Presentation from Thos. Child, Esq., and Certificates from Edward Reynolds, Chr. Fowler, Simon Ford. 17 Nov. 1658.

477. Inckbarrow. John Fyge, 14 Dec. 1658, upon a Presentation from Richard, Lord Protector, and Certificates from Wm. Egerton, James Norman of Lawton, John Poundall of Winslow, Ro. Wallis of Bledlow.

519. Castle Morton, Chappell in the parish of Langdon. Roger Turner, 7 Jan. 1658-9 upon a Presentation from Nicholas Terret, vicar of Langdon, and Certificates from Richard Fincher of All Hallows in Worcester, Ben. Baxter, Tho. Bonnil, Wm. Chetle.

672. Upton Warren. John Hill, M.A., 16 March 1658-9, upon a Presentation from John Talbot, Esq., and Certificates from Giles Collier of Blackley, Jo. Spilsbury, Tho. Bromwich, Geo. Hopkins, Ri. Fincher.

50. Earls Croome. Richard Fletcher, 22 April, 1659, upon a Presentation from William Jeffery, gentleman, and Certificates from Ri. Briscoe, Rector of Barton-on-the-Heath, John Wilson of Welford, Ralph Nevill of Emlead, Rob. Wickens of Todenham, Jo. Easton of Batsford.

54. Hampton Chappell. Thomas Matthewes, 22 Apr., 1659, upon Presentation from the Dean and Chapter of Christ Church, Oxford, and Certificates from Richard Cooper of Weston, Robert Wickens of Toddenham, John Easton of Batteford, Geo. Hopkins of Evesham, Giles Collier of Blackley, Jo. Dolphin of Honiborne, John Trebell of Church Lench.

III.

The Ejected Ministers of Worcestershire, 1660-1662.

T appears from NASH that from 1660 to 1663 there were above sixty Inductions to livings in this county, besides the forty-eight places named below. Hence it is highly probable that a careful investigation would prove the number of ejected ministers in Worcestershire, 1660-1662, much greater than we have hitherto account of.

(BAXTER AND CALAMY'S LISTS.)

Kings Norton   **Thomas Hall, B.D.,*** born in the City of Worcester, 1610, of Oxford, five times imprisoned. Died April 13, 1665.

Moseley   ...   **Joseph Cooper,** son of Hugh Cooper, minister at Preston, Salop. Once he lay in Worcester gaol for the great crime of preaching. Died 1699, aged 74.

City of Worcester ...   St. Andrews, **Joseph Baker.***

* Names thus marked are specially mentioned in *Reliquiæ Baxterianæ*.

	St. Peters	Simon Moore.*
	St. Michaels	
	St. Martins, **Thomas Juice.***
	All Saints	**Richard Fincher.***
	Nicholas	
Kidderminster	**Richard Baxter.**
Kempsey	**Thomas Bromwich.***
Upton-upon-Severn	**Benjamin Baxter.***
Harvington	**Stephen Baxter,*** his brother.
Evesham	All Saints, **George Hopkins,*** **M.A.** Died 1666.
	St. Lawrence, **Thomas Matthews.**
Martley	**Ambrose Sparry,*** for a while maliciously laid in gaol.
Bewdley ...	**Henry Osland,*** **M.A.,** Trin. Coll. Camb.
Old Swinford	**Jarvis Bryan,*** brother to Dr. Ryan of Coventry.
Stone ...	**Richard Serjeant.*** Before, Baxter's assistant.
Bromsgrove	**John Spilsbury, M.A.***
Churchill	**Edward Boucher.***
Chadesly ...	**Thomas Baldwin, senr.*** Died 1693.
All Church ...	**Richard Moore.**
Witley	**Joseph Read ***
Salwarpe	**Richard Wooley,** also his brother **Giles Wooley.**
Cropthorn ...	**William Westmacott.**
White Lady Aston...	**Robert Brown.**
Rydmerley ...	**William Kimberley.**
Eckington ...	**Timothy Jordan.**
Hampton Lovett ...	**John Freeston.**
Doderhill	**Thomas Francis.**
Broadway ...	**John Wall.**
Poppleton ...	Cornelius Woodward.
Huddington	**John Ward.**

* Names thus marked are specially mentioned in *Reliquiæ Baxterianæ.*

Bredon ...	Richard Beeston.
Tredington...	William Durham.
Naunton	Thomas Franks.
Lindridge	John Giles, his father Incumbent.

John Wowen, Chaplain to Lord Ward, ⎫ Trinity
Coll.,
Richard Cooke, ,, Philip Foley, ⎭ Cam.

Stoke ...	Richard Dowley.
Broom	Humphrey Waldern, Baxter's Assistant after Serjeant.
Womborne...	Wilsby.
Clent ...	Andrew Tristram and Thos. Baldwin, junr.
Alvely ...	Lovel, Schoolmaster at Wolverley.

Ejected, but Conforming Afterwards.

Hartlebury...	Thomas Wright.
Wolverley	Simon Potter.
Grafton ...	Hyatt.
Mitton ...	Thos. Soley.
Church Lench ...	Joseph Treble.

Collections for the Distressed Piedmontese Protestants, 1655, in the several parishes of England and Wales.

Record Office, S.P. Dom. Interregnum, I. 126. fol. 263–269.

Co. of Worcester—	£	s.	d.		£	s.	d.
Astley	3	14	4	Bricklehampton ...	0	7	0
Abberley ...	1	4	10	Badsey and Adlington	1	11	11
Arely Kings...	1	13	8	Berrow	2	10	8
Abbotsley ...	1	4	0	Blockley	3	3	11

	£	s.	d.		£	s.	d.
Birlingham ...	1	13	0	Himbleton ...	0	18	8
Bishampton...	0	12	10	Holt	0	15	0
Broadways ...	0	7	8	Hagley ...	1	1	10
Bromsgrove...	10	6	6	Hanley Castle	2	10	0
Broadway	4	5	6	Hartlebury ...	5	0	11
Bayton	0	11	4	Kiderminster	33	16	4
Bockleton	1	14	2	Kings Norton	8	3	10
Belbroughton	2	7	7	Knighton	0	11	10
Breedon	0	13	5	Kyard Wyard	0	14	7
Bewdley, see Ribsford				Lenchwick ...	0	12	6
Bushley	0	13	11	Lindridg ...	1	10	0½
Claines	1	18	2	Lindrich	1	10	0½
Comerton, Little	0	8	6	St. Michaels in Bed-			
,, Great	0	7	7	wardine ...	6	1	1½
Clinton-on-Teme	4	0	6	Martley	1	19	2
Crowle ...	0	10	11	Malvern			
Castell Moreton	0	12	0	Overbury	1	10	8
Credenhill	1	4	0	Parshore—			
Clifton-on-Teme	4	1	1	St. Andrew	4	15	3
Dudley	3	0	3	Holy Crosse	2	15	9
Eckington ...	1	14	10	Peopleton ...	0	8	3
Embley Castle	1	3	9	Piddle North	0	5	3
Estham	1	18	10	Pendock	0	12	0
Evesham—				Pirton	0	17	3
Lawrence...	4	18	6	Pensocks	0	5	10
All Saints...	10	15	7	Ribsford and Bewdley	32	7	3
Bengworth	2	3	9	Ridmarley Dabitot...	1	13	4
Fecknam	0	19	10	Rushock	1	5	6
Fredington	5	9	2	Redmore	0	9	2
Grimley with Fellaw	1	11	3	Rock	3	5	7
Grafton Flyford ...	0	19	8	Rouslench ...	2	3	6

	£	s.	d.		£	s.	d.
Stowlton ...	0	8	11	White Ladyes Aston	3	0	0
Stoke Prior	4	9	5	Warndon	0	9	0
Stourbridge... ...	17	5	7	Woolverly	4	17	2
Stamford-on-Teame	1	0	0	Wickhamford ...	0	18	11
Shelsey Beaucham...	1	15	3	Witley Magna ...	1	13	8
Severn Stoke ...	2	6	10	WORCESTER CITTY—			
Stockton ...	1	3	2	St. Swithin's	4	0	0
Shrawly	2	0	7	Martin's ...	3	13	4
Stanton ...	0	12	0	St. Peter's	4	2	9
Throgmorton	0	5	10	All Saints	8	15	1½
Teambury ...	1	14	5	Hellen	2	11	8
Upton-on-Severn ...	5	9	3				

THE QUAKERS DURING THE COMMONWEALTH.

BESSE, *History of Quakers*, II. 50. Worcestershire, Evesham : Humphry Smith and Thomas Cartwright are imprisoned for refusing to swear. George Hopkins, the minister, pleaded that they refused to swear for tenderness of conscience. The Quakers made a representation to Cromwell describing their cruel treatment. But when brought before the magistrates they kept their hats on, for which offence they were sent back to prison. Among them was Edward Pitway, a magistrate. The fines were afterwards taken off and the prisoners discharged by order of the Protector, Sept. 1, 1655.

Thomas Goodaire for speaking to Richard Baxter after he had ended his sermon at Worcester, was sent to prison, p. 60. Richard Farnsworth was haled out of the steeplehouse at Worcester for asking the said Ri. Baxter a sober question. 1657, Thomas Allington going into one of the places of public worship where he stood still and spake not a word, was taken out and set in the stocks. Edward Bourne for exhorting the people in the College at Worcester to fear the Lord and repent was committed to prison where he remained thirteen weeks. Robert Widder for speaking the words of truth to Richard Baxter in the steeplehouse at Kidderminster, was imprisoned there. [Baxter tells us that the Quakers at this time went naked through the streets, and entering the churches during service, shouted abusively up the aisles, calling the minister deceiver, hireling, liar. For this they were imprisoned; but, on this ceasing, the ministers petitioned to repeal the penal laws against them. See Calamy's *Life of Baxter*, pp. 29, 102, 670. Neal's *History*, IV. 34, 319.]

Major Wilde with party of soldiers going from Evesham to Worcester Dec. 31, 1662, drove Richard Walker, a poor sickly man above 60, before their horses on foot, and when he was not able to keep pace a soldier took and dragged him along by force; the Major himself beat him down with his horse and threatened to pistol him. At length they set him on horseback, whipping the horse both up hill and down hill to the great pain of the infirm man who, when he entreated them to be more merciful to his weak body, met with nothing from them but scoffs and derision. He was thus brought by them to Worcester gaol, but the hardships he had met with by the way had so weakened his body that he died in a short time after his commitment. He was a man of a meek, innocent and Christian spirit, inoffensive in life and conversation, and generally well beloved by those that knew him.—Besse II. 68.

IV.

Names of Places of Meeting and Preachers licenced under the INDULGENCE of Charles II. in the year 1672.

S.P. Domestic Interregnum 38a.

COUNTY OF WORCESTER.

Spilsbury Congr., Bromsgrove.—License toe John Spilsbury to be a Congreg. Teacher in his howse in Bromsgrove, Worcester, 19 Apr., 72.

Bromsgrove Congr., Spilsbury's howse.—The howse of John Spilsbury in Bromsgrove, licensed for a Congr. Meeting Place, 19 Apr., 72.

Bromsgrove Congr. Blick's howse.—Like for the howse of Nicholas Blick in Bromsgrove, Worcester, 19 Apr., 72. Congr.

Above from Domestic Entry Book. In the loose papers is found the following which appears to be a granted application :—

Mr. John Spilsbury, Teacher of the Congregationall perswasion at Bromsgrove in Worcestershire.

The meeting place, at his own house, and at Mr. Nicholas Blicks hous, neer adjoyning, and if it may be, at Mr. William Tytts house also, wch lies neer.

Moore Pr. Weathercock Hill.—License to Richard Moore to be a Pr. Teacher in his howse at Weathercock hill, Worcestershire. 22 Apr., 72.

Weathercock hill Pr. Moores howse.—The house of Rich. Moore of Weathercock hill, Worcestershire, licensed to be a Pr. Meeting Place. 22 Apr., 72.

Licence to Thomas Badland to be a Pr. Teacher in the howse of Wm. Cheatle in Worcester.

The howse of Wm. Cheatle in Worcester, Pr. Meeting Place.

Licence to Rich. Fincher to be a Congr. teacher in the howse of Rich. Cornton in Worcester.

The howse of Rich. Cornton in Worcester Pr.

Licence to Jos. Read to be a Pr. Teacher in Stambridge, Worcester.

The howse of John Read in Stambridge, Worcester.

The howse of Giles Lawrence at Broadway, Worc., Congr.

Licence to John Westmakote to be a Congr. Teacher in Giles Lawrences *sic* at Broadway, Worcester.

The howse of Thomas Worden at Broadway, Worc., Congr. Licence to Thomas Worden to be a Congr. Teacher in his howse at Broadway, Worc.

The howse of Eliz. Stirrup in Worcester, Pr., 22 July. Licence to Rich. Woolly to be a Pr. Teacher in the howse of Eliz. Stirrup in Worcester. 22 July.

The howse of Jos. Cooper in Kingsnorton, Worc. Pr. 22 July. Licence to Joseph Cooper to be a Pr. teacher in his howse at Kingsnorton, Worc. 22 July.

The howse of Edward Rosse at Sukley, Worcester, Pr., 22 July.

Licence to Geo. Wright to be a Pr. Teacher in his own howse at Kingnorton, Worc. 22 July.

The howse of Geo. Wright at Kingsnorton, Worc., Pr. 22 July.

[The howse of Tho. Chapman at Whittington, Warw. Bapt., 25 July. Licence to Manasses King to be an Anab. Teacher in the howse of Thomas Chapman at Whitington, Warw. 25 July.]

Licence to Jarvis Bryan to be a Pr. teacher in his howse at Old Swinford, Worcester, 25 July

The howse of Jarvis Bryan at Old Swinford, Worc. 25 July.

Licence to Rich. Serjeant to be a Pr. teacher in his howse in Hagley, Worc. 25 July.

The howse of Widow Smirt at Everstame, [Evesham] Worc., Congr., 25 July.

The howse of Hen. Osland at Bewdley, Worc. Licence to Henry Osland to be a Pr. Teacher in his howse at Bewdley, Worc. 25 July.

The howse of Rd. Berkes at Old Swinford, Worc., Pr. 25 July.

Like for the howse of Rd. Serjeant at Hagley, Worc., 25 July 72.

The howse of Margery Milward att Dudley in Worc., July 25th 72.

The howse of Fran. Trebell at Bartington, Worc., Congr., 25 July.

Like for the howse of Hen. Osland at Bewdley, Worc., Pr., 25 July.

Like for a Meeting house adjoyning the dweling house of Richard Moore in Kingsnorton in Worcestershire. August 12.

Like for the house of Richard Moore in Kingsnorton, Worcestersh. Au. 12.

Licence to Tho. Baldwin to be a pr. Teach. att Kiderminster in Wo ster sh. Augt. 10th.

The house of Tho. Jeare att Kiderminster in Worcestershire pr Augt. 10th.

The house of Tho. Baldwin of Kiderminster in Worcestersh., pr. Augt. 10.

[Next to this comes " John Bond's house at " Broomyard," Hereford.]

The house of Wm. Greene of Easam in Worcestersh., pr. Augt. 10th.

The house of Tho. Ingold of Hony Bourne in Worcestersh., pr. Sept. 5th.

The house of ye Widd. Westowood of Broomesgrove in Worcestersh. Congr.

The house of Tho. Ingle of Honeybourne in Worcestersh., Congr.

Licence to Rich. Wolley to be a pr. teach. att his owne house in the Citty of Worcester, Sept. 30th.

The house of John Langford of Kierwood in Worcestersh. Anabaptist.

The house of Nicholas Blick of Broomesgrove Worcestersh., Congr. Sept. 30. Licence to John Spilsbury to be a Congr. Teacher, Bromesgrove, Worcestersh.

The house of Rich. Woolley of ye Citty of Worcestersh., pr. Sept. 30th.

Licence to David Jones to be a Congr. Teacher at his owne house at at Dudlew [first written Dudley and then corrected] in ye County of Salop Sept. 30th.

The house of Rich. Smith of ye Citty of Worcester, pr. Nov. 18th 72.

The house of Edw. Robins of Crapthorne in Worcestersh.

The house of Blick of Broomsgrove, Worcestersh, pr. Dec. 9th.

Licence to W. Randall Congr. Teachr. at his owne house att Ombersly in Worcestersh. Decembr. 9th.

The house of Ann Sworle of ye Citty of Worcester, Pr. Dec. 9, 1672.

V.

List of Non-Parochial Registers and Records deposited in Somerset House, in the custody of the Registrar-General.

N the 13th Sept. 1836, Commissioners were appointed to inquire into the state, custody, and authenticity of Non-Parochial Registers and Records; and they sent letters of inquiry to the various churches in England and Wales, requesting information, and suggesting the transfer of the documents to Somerset House, on the plea of safe custody and facility of access. The request was optional, and many declined to part with their registers, in particular the Roman Catholics and the Jews. The majority, however, of Protestant Dissenters through their ministers and other officers complied and deposited their Registers and other Records to be in the custody of the Registrar-General for greater security, legal validity, and easy reference. The documents in question are very numerous, and very valuable, as containing information regarding the successive ministers of the several churches, and in some instances minutes of church meetings, and intimations of interesting facts in the history of our churches.

Down to 1889, access free of charge was enjoyed by properly accredited persons to search and make extracts from these registers for historical and literary purposes; and the present writer, from 1860 downwards, has from time to time availed himself of this obvious right. But in 1889 he received a letter from the Registrar-General refusing free access on the plea of want of necessary accommodation for applicants. The matter was brought before the House of Commons, and Mr. J. CARVELL WILLIAMS, M.P. asked the Government to make representations to the Registrar-General to restore the facilities for many years enjoyed. On May 30, 1895, it was announced in Parliament that "the Registrar-General has made arrangements for the accommodation of any gentleman whose application is backed by an introduction by any M.P. or other well-known person, and who wishes to consult for literary and historical purposes the Non-Parochial Registers and Records which are deposited at Somerset House. No fees will be charged for searching the registers by persons duly accredited." Since this date every facility has been given me, on occasion of my visits, by the chief clerk, Mr. EDWARD WHITAKER. As the printed lists of Non-Parochial Registers and Records (Eyre and Spottiswoode, 1859), are not now to be had, those for the county of Worcester are here given.

No.	Place.	Denomination and Date of Foundation.	Number of Register Books deposited and Description of Entries therein.	What Period extending over.
	WORCESTERSHIRE—			
1	Bewdley	Baptist, 1649.	I. Births ... Deaths and Burials.	1776–1836. 1756–1836.
2	,, High Street ...	Presb. 1696.	I. Births and Baptisms. Burials ...	1722–1823. 1812–1815.
3	Bloomfield	Wesleyan, 1823.	I. Births and Baptisms.	1823–1837.

No,	Place.	Denomination and Date of Foundation.	Number of Register Books deposited and Description of Entries therein.	What Period extending over.
4	Broadway	Independent, 1797.	I. Births and Baptisms.	1801–1837.
5	Bromsgrove, Worcester Street.	Independent and Baptist, 1787.	I. Baptisms Births ...	1788–1804. 1804–1836.
6	Bromsgrove, Chapel Lane, High St., formerly Upper Meeting.	Independent, 1693.	I. Births and Baptisms. II. Births and Baptisms. Burials...	1739–1767. 1770–1837. 1772–1837.
7	Bromsgrove, Little Cat's Hill.	Baptist, 1820.	I. Births ...	1837.
8	Bromsgrove	Wesleyan, 1833.	I. Births and Baptisms. Burials...	1815–1837. 1835–1837.
9	Cradley...	Baptist, 1801.	I. Births and Dedications. Burials...	1809–1836. 1805–1837.
10	,, Park Lane Chapel.	Presb. 1796.	I. Births and Baptisms. II. Births and Baptisms. Burials...	1789–1837. 1818–1837. 1761–1826.
11	Dudley, King Street ...	Independent, 1788.	I. Births and Baptisms.	1803–1837.
12	,, New Street Chapel.	Baptist, 1766.	I. Births ... Deaths...	1816–1837. 1814–1837.
13	,, Wolverhampton Street.	Presb. 1704.	I. Baptisms II. Births and Baptisms. Burials...	1743–1772. 1775–1837. 1831–1835.

No.	Place.	Denomination and Date of Foundation.	Number of Register Books deposited and Description of Entries therein.	What Period extending over.
14	Dudley, King Street ...	Wesleyan, 1788.	I. Births and Baptisms.	1804-1824.
			II. Births and Baptisms.	1824-1837.
15	,, Wolverhampton Street.	Methodist New Connexion, 1829.	I. Burials...	1829-1837.
16	Evesham	Wesleyan, 1813.	I. Births and Baptisms.	1813-1837.
17	,, Oat Street ...	Presb. 1720.	I. Births and Baptisms.	1778-1837.
			Burials...	1822-1836.
18	Feckenham, Astwood Ch. and Alcester, Warwicksh.	Baptist, 1793.	I. Births ...	1788-1837.
			Deaths...	1801-1806.
			II. Burials...	1800-1836.
19	Great Malvern	Countess of Hunt, 1827.	I. Births and Baptisms.	1828 1837.
20	Kidderminster, New Meeting.	Presb. 1872.	I. Births and Baptisms.	1783-1836.
21	,, Old Meeting	Independent, 1662.	I. Baptisms	1727 1822.
			II. Baptisms	1785-1791.
			III. Baptisms	1822-1837.
22	,, Union St. Chapel.	Baptist, 1813.	I. Births ...	1814-1837.
23	,,	Wesleyan.	I. Births and Baptisms.	1788-1811.
			II. Births and Baptisms.	1811-1814.
			III. Births and Baptisms.	1815-1837.

No.	Place.	Denomination and Date of Foundation.	Number of Register Books deposited and Description of Entries therein.	What Period extending over.
24	Kidderminster, Ebenezer Ch.	Countess of Hunt., 1820.	I. Births and Baptisms.	1790–1798.
			II. Births and Baptisms.	1820–1837.
25	,, Sion Field ...	Prim. Meth., 1823.	I. Births and Baptisms.	1833–1837.
26	Leigh Linton and Suckley, also for Cradley in Hereford.	Countess of Hunt., 1818.	I. Births and Baptisms.	1818–1837.
27	Oldbury ...	Wesleyan, 1801.	I. Births and Baptisms.	1832–1837.
			II. Burials...	1823–1836.
			III. Burials...	1836–1837.
28	Redditch	Independent, 1822.	I. Baptisms	1824–1837.
			Burials...	1827–1837.
29	,, &c.	Wesleyan, 1807.	I. Births and Baptisms.	1810–1837.
			II. Births and Baptisms.	1835–1837.
30	Shipston-upon-Stour ...	Baptist, 1778.	I. Births ...	1783–1836.
31	Stourbridge, High Street.	Independent, 1790.	I. Births and Baptisms.	1792–1837.
32	,, ...	Wesleyan, 1800.	I. Births and Baptisms.	1809–1837.
33	Stourport	Wesleyan, 1785.	I. Births and Baptisms.	1788–1813.
			II. Births and Baptisms.	1814–1837.

No.	Place.	Denomination and Date of Foundation.	Number of Register Books deposited and Description of Entries therein.	What Period extending over.
34	Tenbury, Cross Street Chapel.	Baptist, 1816.	I. Births ...	1820–1836.
35	Tipton Green ...	Wesleyan, 1766.	I. Births and Baptisms.	1809–1837.
36	Worcester, Angel St....	Independent, 1668.	I. Baptisms	1699–1759.
			II. Births and Baptisms.	1778–1802.
			Burials...	1783–1793.
			III. Births and Baptisms.	1780–1795.
			IV. Births and Baptisms.	1810–1815.
			V. Births and Baptisms.	1810–1837.
			VI. Burials...	1815–1837.
37	,, Silver St. Ch.	Baptist, 1712.	I. Births ...	1793–1836.
38	,, Pump Street	Wesleyan, 1800.	I. Births and Baptisms.	1803–1837.
39	,, Bridport St.	Countess of Hunt., 1782.	I. Births and Baptisms.	1784–1829.
			II. Births and Baptisms.	1830–1836.

SOCIETY OF FRIENDS—

664	Monthly Meeting of Worcestershire.		Births	1660–1793.
			Marriages	1663–1792.
			Deaths	1666–1793.

665 to 676 Evesham and Alcester.

EXTRACTS.

Worcester, 36 I. Angel Street, Independent, 1699–1759.

(CHEWNING BLACKMORE, Minister, 1699–1737.)

[A small note-book.]

1699.—S. of John Fitzer. Deceased.

1700.—Jan. 16. Ann, d. of Mr. Wm. Swift.

Feb. 16. Jonathan, s. of Mr. John Ryley.

Apr. 4. JOHN, s. of CHEWNING BLACKMORE.

May 6. Elizab. d. of Humphry Wildey. Deceased.

June 5. John, son of Wm. Perkins.

July 24. Hannah, d. of Tho. Jolly. Deceased.

31. Mary, d. of Tho. Cook.

Aug. 1. Hannah, d. of Ja. Haney.

Nov. 26. Elizab., d. to Jos. Tonerson. Deceased.

Dec. 27. William, s. of Nicholas Kent.

1701.—Jan. 1. Mr. HAND baptised a child of —— Griffith, a bastard

Mar. 12 or 13th. Thomas, s. of Tho. Wilsom.

Apr. 7. Joseph, s. of John Pool. Deceased.

8. Hannah, d. of Tom. Mascal, a dyer.

June 30. Anna, d. of Sa. Page.

July 4. James, s. of Benj. Rastall.

Aug. 31. Ann, daughter of J. Ryley. Deceased.

Nov. 18. Tho., s. of Mr. Yardley, glover.

Dec. 1. Isabella, d. of Humphry Wildey. Deceased.

1702.—Jan. 19. Francis, s. of Tho. Smith.

Feb. 12. JONATHAN, s. of JONATHAN HAND. Deceased.

Mar. 15. Elizabeth, d. John Fitzer, clothier.

John, son of   Kennett.

July 23. Mary, d. of Nicho. Kent, by Mr. HAND.

1702.—Aug.	6.	Caleb, s. of Tho. Cook.
	7.	Anna, d. of Mons. De Gerat. Deceased.
	9.	Grace Jolly, d. of Tho. Jolly.
Sept.	30.	Mary, d. of Ri. Randal of Chuckley.
Oct.	2.	Ann, d. of Hen. Bengough. Deceased.
	29.	Elizab., d. of Tim Mascal, by Mr. HAND.
Nov.	2.	Ann, d. of Roger Peirce, at Little Whitley.
		Tho., s. of Tho. Wilsom, by Mr. HAND.
Dec.	13.	John, s. of John Howe, weaver.
1703.—Jan.		James, s. of James Reynolds.
Feb.	12.	Ann, d. of Ja. Harvey.
	16.	Bridget Waring, adult. Deceased.
		Josiah, son of Tho. Smith.
Mar.	29.	Thomas, s. of John Fitzer, clothier.
Apr.	27.	*Francis, s. of Che. Blackmore.*
Aug.	7.	Elizabeth, d. of Tim. Colly.
1704.—July	4.	Margaret, d. of Tho. Cook.
	18.	Elizabeth, d. of Hen. Bengough. Deceased.
Sept.	7.	Joshua, s. of Joshua Avenant.
Oct.	29.	Walter, s. of Ben. Raglal, about this time.
Nov.	30.	Cocker, s. of Cocker Draper. Deceased.
1705.—Jan.	1.	*Edward Chewning, s. of Mr. BLACKMORE.*
		Eliza Child, adult, on ye same day.
Feb.	22.	Mary, d. of Timothy Colles.
	26.	Samuel, s. of Ri. Randall.
Mar.	22.	George, s. of Hen. Bengough.
	30.	Dorothy, d. of Tho. Tolly.
June	22.	Vincent, s. of Wm. Staple.
Aug.	9.	Isabella, d. of Leonard Dark.
	31.	Ann, d. of Hen. Laugher.
Sept.	20.	Joseph, s. of Tho. Cook, Mercer

O

1706.—Aug. 18.   Martha, d. of Edward Cooksey.

Aug. 19 or 26.   of Tho. Smith.

d. of Tim Mascal.

1707.—June   4.   William, s. of William Walbank.   Deceased.

July   6.   Elizabeth, d. of Jas. Harvey.

Sept.   1.   Mary, d. of Joseph Towerson.

5.   Thomas, s. of Henry Bengough.

26.   Wright, s. of Tim. Colles.

Dec.   4.   Edward, s. of Edward Cooksey.

1708.—Feb.   4.   Abigail, d. of Cocker Draper.

Apr. 21.   Ann, d. of Rich. Randall.

27.   Ann, d. of James Linton.

Oct.   2.   Bridget, d. of Henry Laugher.

Nov.   2.   Ann, d. of Edw. Cooksey.

Elizab. d. of James Rainolds.   Deceased.

1709.—July 15.   Anna, d. of Tim. Colles.

17.   John, s. of Rev. Mr. JA. THOMPSON.   Deceased.

25.   Elizabeth, d. of John Trap.

Sept. 14.   *Mary, d. of Ch. Blackmore.*

1710.—Jan. 17.   Cocker, s. of Cocker, Draper.   Deceased.

s. of Wm. Staple.

Mar.   8.   Henry, s. of Henry Bengough.   Deceased.

July 15.   Elizabeth, d. of John Trap.

Oct.   9.   George, s. of Edw. Cooksey.

1711.—Feb.   1.   Sarah, d. of Tim. Colles.   Deceased.

Mar. 17.   Henry, s. of Henry Bengough.

June 10.   SARAH BLACKMORE.

Oct. 18.   William, s. of Jos. Tonerton.

Dec. 12.   Ann, d. of Edw. Cooksey.

1712.—Jan. 13.   Elizabeth, d. of Henry Bengough.

June 12.   d. of Jos. Morley.

July 18.   Samuel, s. of Wm. Amphlet of Ombersley.

1712.—Aug.		Ann, d. of John Ruston.
Oct.	7.	Hannah, d. of John Trap.
Nov.		Comfort, d. of Cocker Draper.
Dec.	9.	Edward, s. of Edw. Cooksey.
		Robert, s. of Williams.
1713.—Jan.	13.	Elizabeth, d. of Henry Bengough.
Feb.	10.	Hanna, d. of Ja. Linton. Deceased.
	17.	Timothy, s. of Tim. Colles.
June	15.	Samuel, s. of Jos. Weaver.
	18.	s. of Geo. Cookey, by Mr. HAND.
Oct.	21.	Hannah, d. of John Savage.
	30.	Mary, d. of Tho. Smith.
Nov.	25.	Jane, d. of Leonard Dark.
1714.—Jan.	16.	Mary, d. of Edw. Cooksey.
Feb.	25.	John, s. of Edw. Trap.
Mar.	30.	Edward, s. of Gibbs, Weaver.
June	15.	Margaret, d. of Cocker Draper.
	22.	Job, s. of John Ruston.
Nov.	30.	Ann, d. of Edw. Lownds.
Dec.	14.	Ann, d. of Wm. Amphlet.
1715.—Feb.	11.	Joice, d. of Edw. Cooksey.
Mar.	1.	William, s. of W Herbert.
Apr.	18.	John, s. } of Goodall.
		Elizabeth, d. }
		Also Tho., s. of Tho. Taylor.
June	3.	Frances, d. of Henry Laugher. Deceased.
July	13.	Henry, s. of Henry Bengough.
	19.	Susannah, d. of Tim. Colles.
1716.—Jan.	25.	Henry, s. of Henry Fitzer, Shoemaker.
Feb.	13.	Martha, d. of John Savage.
Oct.	1.	Mary, d. of Wm. Herbert.
	25.	Francis, s. of Fran. Brook.

1716.—Nov.   3.   Edw., s. of Geo. Cooksey.

             8.   Mary, d. of Tho. Harrison.

    Dec.   1.   Caleb, s. of John Ruston.

1717.—Oct.   21.   John, s. of John Savage, by Mr. HAND.

1721.—Dec.   18.   Tho. Harrison, by Mr. SEDGLEY.

1722.—Mar.   8.   Margaret, d. of Phil. Fincher.

    July   6.   Elizabeth, d. of Mr. Ri. Bradly.

1723.—Jan.   15.   John, s. of George Nelson, a Scotchman.

    May   17.   Mary, d. of Philip Fincher.

1724.—Apr.   12.   John, s. of William Dudfield, by Mr. OSLAND.

1726.—Aug.   29.   Mary, d. of Mr. Ri. Bradley.

    Sept.   1.   Susan, d. of Wm. Price, Joiner, by Mr. THO. PERROT.

1727.—Mar.   6.   Elizab., d. of   Hanbury, at Kederminster.

    Aug.   17.   John Hook, s. of Philip Fincher.

1730.—Mar.   3.   Mary, d. of Mr. John Stokes.

1731.—Oct.   18.   Hesther, d. of David Moore, a North Briton.

    Dec.   17.   *William Wilkes*, s. of FRAN. BLACKMORE.

1733.—June   24.   Gyles, s. of Wm. Hooper, Apothecary.

1735.—Apr.   29.   George, s. of John Hodges, *baptized by* Mr. PERKINS of Bromyard.

    Aug.   16.   Grac, d. of John Carpenter, baptized by Mr. FRANCIS BLACKMORE.

1736.—Jan.   22.   Joseph, s. of Rev. Mr. JOHN STOKES, by Rev. Mr. BARRETT.

    Feb.   15.   William, s. of John Wickett by Rev. Mr. BRADSHAW.

    Feb.   19.   Elizabeth, d. of   Walton, by Mr. BARRETT.

    Mar.   28.   Ann, d. of Roger Stokes, a souldier, by Mr. BARRETT.

    May   23.   William, s. of Mr. Hooper, Apothecary, by Mr. CARPENTER, of Warwick.

1736.—Aug. 8. Leonard, s. of Leonard Dark, by Mr. BARRETT.

9. Ann, d. of Mr. R. Laugher.

[Mr. Chewning Blackmore died 1737.]

A gap of seven years during the Pastorate of the Rev. Francis Spillsbury.

1743.—A list of those baptized by FRANCIS BLACKMORE since my charge of the Christian Society of Protestant Dissenters in Worcester.

1743.—Worcester, April 26, I baptized (at his dwelling-house) ye son of Mr. George Gillam, named Thomas.

Kidderminster, July 4, I baptized the son of John Pearsal, at his dwelling-house, named William.

1743.—Bromsgrove, October 3, I baptized (at his dwelling-house), the son of the Rev. Mr. SAM PHILIPS, named Samuel.

1743.—Kidderminster, December 4, I baptized at his dwelling-house in Mill Street, the dâter of Mr. John Read, name Anna.

1744.—March 8, I baptized (at his dwelling-house, in Sidbury), the son of Mr. Geo. Gorl, baker, named George.

Worcester, Dec. 16, baptized ye son of Mr. Joseph Carter (at his dwelling-house), named Samuel.

1745.—I baptized (at his dwelling-house) the son of Mr. Douglas (Wm.), named William, May 30, 1745.

Aug. 4, the s. of Mr. Wm. Wotton, named James.

Sept. 22, the d. of Mr. Budden, named Elizabeth.

1745.—Bromsgrove, Nov. 11, 1745, I baptized ye son of Rev. Mr. SAMUEL PHILIPS, named Thomas Mann.

Worcester, Dec. 8, baptized the dâter of Mr. Thomas Hammond, named Elizabeth.

1745-6.—Worcester, March 7, I baptized the son of Mr. BENJAM. PERKINS, named William.

The son of Mr. WM. DOUGLAS, named Henry, Dec. 16, 1746.

1747-8.—I baptized Rev. Mr. SAM. PHILIPS's son, of Bromsgrove, at his house there, named Samuel.

[A gap of ten years.]

1758.—June 26, I baptized, at Manchester, in my son W. W. B.'s house, in Radcliff Street, his son, named Robert Grierson. He was born about one o'clock in the morning, on the 12th of June, 1758, at Manchester aforesaid.

(Last entry) :—

April 29, 1759, I baptized (at his dwelling-house, Worcester), the son of Mr. Benjamin Blower, named Thomas.

The above by F. B.—FRANCIS BLACKMORE, 1743-1759.

(Here ends Register 36 I. *Worcester, Angel Street.)*

---

* WORCESTER 36 II.—Births and Baptisms, 1778-1802.

Burials, 1783-1793.

"A REGISTER OF PERSONS BAPTIZED BY THE MINISTERS OF THE CONGREGATION OF PROTESTANT DISSENTERS, ANGEL LANE, WORCESTER."

A REGISTER OF BAPTISMS.

1778.—Oct. 15. Mary, d. of John Fitzer.

1779.—Feb. 1. Robert, s. of Tim. Gillam.

Feb. 15. Thomas, s. of Jacob Stokes.

May 7. Sarah, d. of Henry Hammond.

11. Mary, d. of Webb.

July 4. Thomas, s. of James Holliday.

Aug. 29. Andrew, s. of John Walker.

Oct. 25. Robert, s. of Thomas Rickards, Esq.

1780.—Feb. 15. Thomas, s. of Thomas Jenkins.

Mar. 6. Elizabeth, d. of Robert Taylor.

Apr. 6. William, s. of Wm. Oram.

* Not copied in full.—W. U.

1780.—May 14. Mary, d. of John Powell.

July 19. Hannah, d. of the Rev. Wm. WELLS of Bourn-heath.

Aug. 22. John, s. of Henry Bishop.

Dec. 4. Ann, d. of Thomas Rickards.

22. Richard, s. of Ri. Blower.

1781. Jan. 15. William, s. of John Oliphant.

17. Hannah, d. of Henry Hammond.

Apr. 22. Jane, d. of John Blackwell.

June 25. Henry, s. of Ri. Watson of Kid.

July 18. Elizabeth Venner, d. of John Mayall.

20. Mary, d. of Ch. Brown.

Aug. 9. Phebe, d. of Jacob Stokes.

N.B.—All the fore-mentioned were baptized by the Rev. THOMAS BELSHAM.

Those that follow were baptized by the Rev. Jos. GUMMER.

1781, Nov. 12, to Aug. 18, 1785, forty-three Baptisms in all.

"N.B.—All the fore-mentioned from page 3, and the date of Nov. 12, 1781, to that of the date Aug. 18, 1785 inclusive, were baptized by me, JOSEPH GUMMER."

N.B.—The Register continued on page 13. A threepenny stamp is affixed to each entry.—W. U

1785, Oct. 2, to June 20, 1791, fifty-two entries, four on a page, and each page is signed thus at the foot—

"The above four were baptized by Jos. GUMMER."

1788, May 28, Oliver Cromwell, s. of Oliver Field, Linendraper of the parish of St. Swithin, and Elizabeth his wife, born Apr. 14.

July 23, 1792, signed by *John Barrett.*

Born Feb. 14, 1792, John, son of John Flight, of the parish of St. Swithin, Worc., China manufacturer (deceased July 10, 1791), and Ann his wife. Present at the birth, Ann Russell, midwife ; Mary Ann Lamb, nurse.

John Barrett signs as officiating min. on July 25, 1792
Ministers officiating at further baptisms :—

THOMAS WILLIAMS, Hereford, Sept. 26, 1792.

THOMAS JONES, Jan. 7, 1793.

JOHN DAWSON, Dec. 29, 1793.

JOHN DAWSON, Dec. 30, 1793.

EDWD. WILLIAMS, Jan. 19, 1794.

JOEL BANFIELD, Dec. 31, 1794, and six following entries.

EDW. WILLIAMS, July 31, 1798, Aug. 4, 1798.

JOEL BANFIELD, 1799.

THOS. KING, July 26, 1799.

BURIALS, 1783–1793.

Worcester 36 II. ; at the end of the volume are :—

(1) Ann Rickards, daughter of Thomas Rickards, Esq., of Bevere, in the County of Worcester, and Ann, his wife, was buried in the Meeting-house, June 19, 1781, by the Rev. THOS. BELSHAM.

(2) Hannah, wife of Thos. Hodges Glover, buried in the Meeting-house, Feb 28, 1783.

(3) Joseph, son of Tho. Rickards, Esq., buried Jan. 27, 1785, aged 3 weeks.

(4) Susannah, wife of Henry Hammond, hop merchant, died Oct. 3, was buried Oct. 6, in the Meeting-house, 1786.

(5) Ann Bulford, spinster, died Oct. 16, was buried Oct. 22, 1788, in the yard adjoining the Meeting-house.   Aged 36.

(6) Elizabeth Faulkner, spinster, died Jan. 6, buried Jan. 9, 1789, in the yard adjoining the Meeting-house.   Aged 59.

(7) George Gillam, died June 2, was buried June 10 (1789), in the Meeting-house.   *Aet.* 8.

(8) Elizabeth, wife of Mr. Henry Bishop, woolen-draper, died Oct. 19, was buried Oct. 24, 1789, in the Meeting-house, aged 43.

Mrs. Sarah Stephens, died Jan. 25, 1789, was buried at the Baptist Meeting-house.

(9) Mrs. Frances Hurt, wife of Mr. Joseph Hurt, of Birlingham, Worcester, was buried Dec. 27, 1790, in the Meeting-house.

(10) Mrs. Williams, wife of Mr. Geo. Williams, of Worcester, glover, was buried in the Meeting-house, Feb. 7, 1791.

(11) 1791.—March 24, JOHN DOUGLAS, of the city of Worcester, snuff-maker, died March 19, buried in the Meeting-house, March 24, 1791.

(12) July 20, JOHN FLIGHT, of Worcester, china manufacturer, died July 6, was buried in the Meeting-house, July 20, 1791. Aged 25.

(13) 1793.—March 9, Henry Bishop, of Worcester, woolen-draper, died Sunday, March 3, buried in the Meeting-house, March 9. Per G. OSBORN.

(14) 1793.—March 29, John, son of the late John Flight, of Worcester, china manufacturer, and of Anne, his wife, died March 24, buried in the Meeting-house, March 29, 1793. Aged 13 months. Per G. OSBORN.

(This is the last entry in Worcester 36 H.)

WORCESTER, 36 III.—Births and Baptisms, 1780–1795.

REGISTER OF BAPTISMS IN THE INDEPENDENT SOCIETY OF PROTESTANT DISSENTERS IN THE CITY OF WORCESTER, ASSEMBLING IN PUMP STREET, WORCESTER.

Twenty entries—

1780.—Feb. 1. Mary, d., Thos. and Ann Stokes, baptized by the late Pastor.

1781.—Aug. 8. Maria, d., Wm. Talbot, baptised by Thos. Williams, minister.

1782.—Sept. 18. Thomas, s., Thos. and Ann Stokes, baptized by Thos Williams, minister.

1792.—Oct. 12. John, s., John and Margaret Nairne, born Oct. 9, by me John Lewis, minister.

1793.—Mar. 15. Elizabeth, d. of Oliver and Elizabeth Field, born Feb. 13, 1793, John Lewis, minister of Kingwood.

Mar. 31. John, s. of John and Susanna Cope, born March 3, J. Lewis, minister.

Apr. 14. James, s. of Wm. and Charlotte Scott, 2nd Dragoons, Feb. 4, J. Lewis, minister.

Apr. 22. James, s. of Alex. and Esther Johnstone, sergeant, J. Lewis, minister.

Apr. 26. James, s. of James and Janet Richmond, quartermaster, J. Lewis, minister.

Apr. 28. John Spooner, J. Lewis, minister.

Apr. 28. James, s. of Sam and Susanna Cope, J. Lewis, minister.

1793.—July 21. Ann, d. of Hugh and Elizabeth Dick, corporal, born July 17, J. Lewis, minister.

Ann, d. of Ri. and Mary Stokes, born May 9, J. Lewis, minister.

Sept. 11. Charles Swift, s. of Charles and Marg. Yardley, 16 Aug., J. Lewis, minister.

Dec. 2. Prudence, d. of John and Marg. Nairne, Dec. 1, J. Lewis, minister.

Dec. 30. Mary, d. of Joseph and Alice Ellis, Dec. 28, J. Lewis, minister.

1794.—May 18. Ann, d. of Adam and Elizabeth Glandenning, born May 4, J. Lewis, minister.

July 3. Jane, d. of James and Sarah Steel, born June 11, J. Lewis, minister.

1795.—Jan. 29. Margaret, d. of Charles and Marg. Yardley, born
Dec. 2, 1794, WILL. FIELD, minister.

Jan.   29. John, s. of Oliver and Elizabeth Field, born Nov 2,
1794, WILL. FIELD, minister.

(The end of this register)

WORCESTER 36 IV.—Births and Baptisms, 1810 1815.

"THE REGISTER OF BAPTISMS BELONGING TO THE PROTESTANT DIS-
SENTING CONGREGATION ASSEMBLING IN ANGEL STREET, WORCESTER,
having through some unhappy differences been of late inaccessible, it has
been deemed expedient that a proper list of Baptisms be for the present
inserted in this Book. This is done with a hope that at some future time
this list may be transcribed into the proper Register belonging to the
congregation."

Ann Burden, daughter of Stephen and Elizabeth Burden, born 18 Oct.
1809, baptized 20 July 1810, by SAMUEL LOWELL of Bristol. Worc.
Aug. 1811.

John, the son of RICHARD EVANS of Haughton, Montgomeryshire, and
Esther his wife of Kidderminster, born 1st July 1811, and baptized
Aug. 27, 1811, by me, ALEX. STEILL of Wigan.

Elizabeth, d. of Stephen and Elizabeth Burden of Worcester, born
March 1, 1811, baptized 27 Aug. 1811 by me, ALEX. STEILL of
Wigan.

Thomas, son of Stephen and Elizabeth Burden of Worcester, born
Apr. 19, 1812, baptized Apr. 29, 1813 by me, JOHN HARRIS of
Whitechurch.

Hannah, daughter of Thomas and Hannah Evans, born Jan. 26, 1811,
baptized Apr. 29, 1813 by me, JOHN HARRIS of Whitechurch.

Eliza, daughter of Thomas and Hannah Evans, born June 29, 1812,
baptized Apr. 29, 1813 by me, JOHN HARRIS of Whitechurch.

Esther, daughter of Stephen and Elizabeth Burden, born Dec. 7, 1813, baptized Jan. 31, 1814 by me, JOHN HARRIS of Whitechurch.

Frederick Felton, son of Robert and Elizabeth Felton, hop merchant, born 5 Apr. 1801, baptized by the Rev. Mr. BAMFIELD of Bromyard.

Elizabeth, daughter of Robert and Elizabeth Felton, born 11 Nov. 1808, baptized by the Rev. Mr. STEEL of Kidderminster.

Catharine, daughter of Robert and Elizabeth Felton, born Jan. 1, 1812, baptized Apr. 24, 1812.   D. FLEMING.

Lucy, daughter of John Young, glover, bapt. 28 Oct. 1814.   D. FLEMING.

Mary, daughter of Thomas and S. Evans, born March 21, 1814, baptized Nov. 14, 1814.   D. FLEMING.

William Henry, son of William Henry and Mary Woods, born 8 Dec. 1814, baptized 17 Dec. 1814.   D. FLEMING.

James, son of John and Mary Morton, born Jan. 1815, baptized Jan. 1815. D. FLEMING.

Susanna, daughter of Stephen and Elizabeth Burden, born 16 Jan. 1815, baptized Oct. 1, 1815, by WM. POTTER, Protestant Dissenting Minister.

(The end of this Register.—W. U.)

WORCESTER 36 V.

36 V. (a large handsome folio in vellum).—Births and Baptisms, 1810–1837.

BIRTHS, BAPTISMS AND BURIALS, IN ANGEL STREET MEETING HOUSE OF THE INDEPENDENT DENOMINATION ; deposited Jan. 30, 1837.

GEORGE REDFORD, D.D., L.L.D., Minister.

RICHD. EVANS, } Trustees and Deacons.
STEPHEN BURDEN, }

It begins with those entries given above in 36 IV. from July 20, 1810, to Oct. 1, 1815.

Then—

1816, March 10, Esther, daughter of Richard and Esther Evans, (late Cooper, spinster), grocer, Broad Street, Worc., born Jan. 9, 1816, baptized by J. A. James, of Birmingham.

1816, March 10, Sarah, daughter of Thomas and Sarah Morgan, (late Whitfield spinster), baker, Bridge Street, born Jan. 8, 1816, baptized by J. A. James, of Birmingham.

1816, March 10, William Henry, son of William Henry and Margaret Woods (late Baxter, spinster), painter, born Feb. 18, 1816, baptized by J. A. James, of Birmingham.

*   *   *   *   *

1824, June 28, Robert Alfred, born March 18, 1823, son of Robert Vaughan and Susanna (late Ryall, spinster, Melcombe Regis, Dorset), pastor of the Church in Angel Street, baptized by George Clayton.

[N.B.—The officiating ministers signing the register are :—J. A. James ; John Berry ; John Richards, Stourbridge ; Joseph Turnbull, of Cainscross, Gloucestershire ; William Lane, of Wells, Somerset ; Robert Vaughan, from Dec., 1822 to May 22, 1824. George Clayton ; John Roaf ; George Redford, Jan. 15, 1826–Oct. 31, 1837.—W. U.]

Worcester 36, VI.

36 VI.—Burials, 1815–1837.

In 1823–1824 signed by Robt. Vaughan.

1826, Oct., signed by Geo. Redford, and by him onwards to Aug. 23, 1837.

Worcester 37.   Silver Street.—Births 1793–1836.

Register Book of Births kept in Silver Street Baptist Chapel, Worcester, founded 1712. The chapel now standing was built 1797. "The Register has been in the custody for some time of Mr. Samuel

Daniel, Deacon, and is sent from the immediate custody of THOMAS WATERS of Hylton Street, Worcester, who has kept it for some time past as the minister. Sept. 12, 1837."

First entry :—Aug. 30, 1793. James Nichalls, son of Samuel and Ann, registered by me, WILLIAM BELSHER, Minister of Silver Street Meeting, Worcester. SAMUEL DANIELL, son of Saml. and Mary, born May 10, 1800, "registered by me HENRY PAGE, Pastor of the Church in Silver Street, Worcester," and then follows Elizabeth, Mary, Charles, Luiza, Emily, Daniell, Oct. 22, 1804, " by me, HENRY PAGE, Pastor of the Church in Silver Street, Worcester."

"The foregoing registers were copied from Mr. Saml. Daniell's Family Bible, with some additional circumstances communicated personally by Mr. and Mrs. Daniell to HENRY PAGE. The above statement is correct :—Samuel Daniell, Father, Mary Daniell, Mother. Witness to the signatures, *Emily Daniell.*"

RICHARD BAUGH DAY, 25 Dec. 1795
Catherine Day, born 28 May 1797   Regd. by me, HENRY PAGE, Pastor
Millicent Day   ,,   5 Jan. 1805   of the Church in Silver Street.
Elizabeth Day   ,,   30 Apr. 1807

ELIZABETH SCANDRETT, born Aug. 31, 1797
Milborough Scandrett   ,,   Nov. 8, 1803   Regd. by me, HENRY
Charles Scandrett   ,,   Jan. 30, 1805   PAGE, Pastor of the
Mary Scandrett   ,,   Sept. 15, 1809   Church in Silver Street.
Alfred Scandrett   ,,   June 12, 1814

Henry Davis, born July 7, 1796   Registered by me, HENRY PAGE.
James Davis   ,,   July 16, 1803

BENJ. PRICE, born 25 Mar. 1798   Regd. by me HENRY PAGE, minister
William Price, born 19 Oct. 1799   of Silver Street Meeting, Wor-
John Price, born   cester.
Edward Price, born 21 Dec. 1803

John Kenyon Blackwell, born 14 Sept. 1812		
Sam. Holden Blackwell, ,, 8 May 1816		Regd. by me HENRY
Martha Dufty ,, 20 Sept. 1806		PAGE, minister of
Hannah Dufty ,, 12 July 1809		Silver Street Meet-
Sarah Dufty ,, 30 Nov. 1812		ing, Worcester.
Robert Dufty ,, 15 Jan. 1815		
William Dufty ,, 27 Jan. 1817		

Catherine Osborn Pitt	Daughter of	July 11, 1815	Regd. by me
Fanny Hartley	Joseph and	Aug. 12, 1816	HENRY PAGE.
Sarah	Cath. Pitt.	Dec. 15, 1817	

Edwin Edmonds Rouse		Born 17 Dec. 1809	Registered by
John Henry Rouse		,, 6 Feb. 1811	me HENRY
Emma Rouse	Children	,, 15 Feb. 1812	PAGE, minis-
Caleb Thomas Rouse	of John	,, 9 Aug. 1813	ter of Silver
William Felix Rouse	and Sarah	,, 2 Sept. 1815	Street Meet-
Eliza Ann Rouse	Rouse.	,, Oct. 1816	ing, Worces-
James Rouse		,, 7 Dec. 1817	ter.

HENRY PAGE, son of JOHN and ELIZABETH PAGE, born Mar. 19, 1781.

SARAH ANN SELFE, daughter and only surviving child of James and Ann
Selfe, was born at Trowbridge, March 1, 1780.

Henry Page and Sarah Ann Selfe were married at Trowbridge, 29th June
1802, and have had issue as follows :—

1.—Sarah Ann Selfe Page, born in the parish of St. Paul, Bristol,
1 Sept. 1803.

2.—Emily Selfe Page, born in the parish of St. Paul, Bristol, 19 Dec.
1804.

3.—Eliza Selfe Page, born in the parish of St. Paul, Bristol, 27 Sept.
1806, died in London, July 22, 1811.

4.—Mary Selfe Page, born in the parish of St. Paul, Bristol, 25 June 1808.

5.—Henry James Selfe Page, born at Bristol, 15 Nov. 1810.

6.—Anna Eliza Selfe Page, born at Bristol, 3 July, 1812.

7.—Alfred Selfe Page, born at Bristol, 5 July 1814, died Dec. 24, 1815

8.—Caroline Selfe Page, born at Bristol, 16 Oct. 1816.

9.—Ellen Selfe Page, born at Worcester, 4 Sept. 1819.

10.—James Selfe Page, born at Worcester, 18 Sept. 1821.

Registered by me, HENRY PAGE, minister of Silver Street Meeting, Worcester, and father of the children above mentioned.

[Last entry by Henry Page, 27 Jan. 1826. THOMAS WATERS, minister, signs Feb. 1837. Last entry Sept. 5, 1837.]

WORCESTER 39 I. Births and Baptisms, 1784-1829.

THE REGISTER BOOK OF BAPTISMS AT THE COUNTESS OF HUNTINGDON'S CHAPEL, BIRDPORT STREET, WORCESTER.

Thos. Yeels, son of Wm. and Elizabeth Yeels, baptized Oct. 24, 1784 by SAML. BEAUFOY.

Susanna Yeels, d. of Wm. and Eliz. Yeels, baptized Mar. 24, 1788 by JOHN CHILD.

Nancy, d. of Thos. and Mary Carradine, baptized Apr. 7, 1788 by JOHN CHILD.

Thomas, s. of John and Ann Morgan, baptized Apr. 14, 1788 by JOHN CHILD.

John, s. of James and Jane Grob, baptized May 8, 1788 by JOHN CHILD.

Joseph, s. of Wm. and Martha Macklane, May 18, 1788 by JOHN CHILD.

William, s. of Bate and Mary Penn, baptized July 18, 1788, WM. COLLINS.

The Register is signed by several occasional ministers down to 1806. Then Rev. Edw. Lake begins, and his signature appears from 1810 to 1829.

Worcester 39 II.   Births and Baptisms, 1830-1836.

Almost all the entries are signed by Edward Lake.

"The Rev. Edward Lake has kept the Books since 1810, and now holds them as minister, May 2, 1837.   We have a Register Book from Kidderminster which is herewith sent."

WORCESTERSHIRE 21 I.

KIDDERMINSTER OLD MEETING HOUSE, INDEPENDENT, 1662.

I.—Baptisms, 1727-1822.

II.—Baptisms, 1785-1791.

III.—Baptisms, 1822-1837.

AN ACCOUNT OF BAPTISMS IN THE CONGREGATION OF BAPTIZED PROTESTANT DISSENTERS IN KIDDERMINSTER, 1727, Sept. 25 to Apr. 1, 1742.

The above account is the Rev. Mr. BRADSHAW'S, and ended with his life.

A register of persons baptized by *B. Fawcett* chiefly in Kidderminster, but other places are expressly named.

1753, Feb. 13, Elizabeth, d. of Ri. and Rebecca BADLAND.

1755, Sept. 9, Lucy, d. of Richard and Rebecca BADLAND.

1757, Nancy } Twins of Ri. and Rebecca BADLAND.
Phebe

1780, July 11, last entry of B. FAUCETT.

1779, Aug. 16-1781 Mar. 13, thirteen by R. PARMINTER.

N.B.—In 1781 baptism by MORRIS, STEPH. ADDINGTON, JOHN LAKE, THOS. BELSHAM, THOS. TAYLOR, JOHN BERRY, BENJ. DAVIES, THOS. WILLIAMS, JAS. WRAITH.

Baptisms by JOHN BARRETT, 1782-1797.

1798, Baptisms by ALEX. STEILL.

P

Joshua, son of Joshua Smith of Worcester, and Ann his wife, of Kempsey, near Worcester, born Jan. 10, 1798, baptized Nov. 2, 1798.

1801, Robert, son of ALEX. STEILL, of Gosport, Hants, and Mary his wife, of Winchester, born Oct. 31, 1800, baptized Feb. 3, 1801 by me, THOS. GARDNER.

EDWARD, son of JOHN EVANS, of St. Chad's, Shrewsbury, and Mary his wife, born Jan. 31, 1801, baptized July 4, 1801.

Samuel, son of ALEX. STEILL, born May 26, 1803, baptized July 11, 1803, by me, JOHN BERRY.

THOMAS HELMORE, minister, July 18, 1810.

JOSEPH JOHN FREEMAN, 1820–1822.   Afterwards missionary in Madagascar with the Rev. Mr. JOHNS.

KIDDERMINSTER OLD MEETING, INDEPENDENT.

WORCESTERSHIRE 21, II.—Births and Baptisms.

JOHN BARRETT, min. 1785–1792.

WORCESTER 21, III.   KIDDERMINSTER.

"The books have been sent by the Minister, who has kept them since 1827.   ROBERT ROSS, 10 April, 1837.

SOCIETY OF FRIENDS, WORCESTERSHIRE, 664.

" SEE MERCY, son of George and Susan Adams, born in the parish called
    St. Clement, ye 18th day of ye 6th month, 1660.

P. 5.—Mary, d. of Francis and Mary Fincher, born 28th of 1st month,
    1680.

Francis, son of Francis and Mary Fincher, born 15th of 1st mo. 1680–1.

MARRIAGES, *e.g.*

"The 25th day of 11th month, 1663, JOHN WAIGHT took ELIZABETH READ to wife in ye presence of us whose names are under written,

Thomas Jenkins,	Abraham Armes,	Mary Amphleet,
Ri. Fidoe,	Thos. Ball,	Mary Jenkins,
Edw. Stanton,	Ro. Smith,	Margaret Roberts,
Abraham Roberts,	Elizabeth Smith,	Mary Hill.

FRANCIS FISCHER took MARY ACHELLY, to wife 3rd day of 4th month, 1678. In presence of

Wm. Pardoe,	Richd. Bott,	Joyce Jefferyes.
Rob. Smith,	Alex. Beardsley,	Mary Pardoe,
Geo. Maris,	Job Waring,	Alice Maris,
Tho. Reeves,	John Love,	Milliscent Hodgkins.

[*These registers are very copious and remarkably well kept.*—W.U.]

RETURN.—CHURCHES, CHAPELS, AND BUILDINGS FOR RELIGIOUS WORSHIP.

(Ordered by the House of Commons to be printed, 15 November 1882.)

Places of Worship certified under Acts 15 & 16 Vict. c. 36, and 18 & 19 Vict. c. 81.* Registration District of WORCESTER.

Name.	*Where situate.*	*Religious Denomination.*
Mr. Haskew's large Room.	Carden Street, Worcester.	Latter Day Saints.
A Building	Boughton Street, Saint John's in Bedwardine.	Wesleyan Methodists.

* Places of Worship certified prior to 1st July 1852 do not appear in this list unless subsequently certified to the Registrar-General under the above-named Acts.

Name.	*Where situate.*	*Religious Denomination.*
Saint John's Chapel ...	Pump Street, Saint Helen, Worcester.	Wesleyan Methodists.
Friends' Meeting House.	Sansome Fields, Worcester.	Friends.
A Building ...	In Bull Entry, Saint Swithin, Worcester.	Wesleyan Reformers.
St. George's Catholic Chapel.	Sansome Place, Worcester.	Roman Catholics.
Zion Chapel	Park Street, Blockhouse	Wesleyan Methodists Association.
Congregational Chapel	Angel Street	Independents.
Primitive Methodist Chapel.	South Street, Blockhouse, Worcester.	Primitive Methodists.
Lady Huntingdon's Free Church.	Birdport Street, Worcester.	Lady Huntingdon's Connexion.
Baptist Chapel ...	Sansome Walk ...	Baptists.
Brethren's Meeting Room.	Nicholas Street, Worcester.	Brethren.
Ebenezer Chapel ...	Swineshead ...	Protestant Dissenters.
Countess of Huntingdon's Chapel.	Lowesmoor	Countess of Huntingdon's Connexion.
Music Hall ...	Old Corn Market, Worcester.	Evangelization Society.
Mission Hall ...	Wyld's Lane, Worcester.	Who object to be designated.
Working Man's Hall	Silver Street, Worcester.	Protestants.
Berkeley Room ...	Shaw Street, Worcester	Who object to be designated.
Christ Church	Castle Street, Worcester.	Presbyterian Church of England.

Name.	Where situate.	Religious Denomination.
Christians' Meeting Room.	St. Nicholas Street, Worcester.	Christians.
Baptist Chapel	Red Hill, Worcester ...	Baptists.
Concert Hall ...	Lowesmoor	Salvation Army.
Baylis's School Room	Cherry Tree Walk, Infirmary Walk, Worcester.	Who object to be designated.

CONGREGATIONS IN WORCESTERSHIRE, *circ.* 1715.

(Morrice MSS., Dr. Williams' Library.)

N.B.—C. = City, or county town ; B.T. = Borough town ; M. = Market town ; P. = Presbyterian ; I. = Independent ; A. = Anabaptist ; B. = Baptist ; H. = Hearers.

Place of Meeting.	Preachers.	Hearers.
Worcester, C. ...	Chewning Blackmore, John Stokes, 1720. Hand Dec. 1719 P.	700
Evesham, B.T.	Daniel Higgs, died Oct. 1728. F. Blackmore, 1728. P.	200
Bewdley, B.T.	Edward Oasland, Job Barret. P.	300
Bromsgrove, M. ...	James Thompson, died Nov., 1729. P. ...	400
Kiderminster, M. ...	John Spilsbury, died 1727. Bradshaw, 1727. P.	—
Dudley, M.	Joseph Stokes. Pf.	—
Sturbridge, M.	George Flower, ordained Apr. 14, 1698. P.	—
Westmercote, near Tewkesbury.	William Ferris. I.	40

Place of Meeting.	Preachers.	Hearers.
Kingswood in ye parish of Kings' Norton.	By several ; especially by Wotton. Pf. ...	—
Worcester, C.	Pointing. A. ...	400
Bewdley, B.T.	William Thompson. A.	100
Parshore, M.	Timothy Thomas, died Jan., 1716-7. A. Timothy Thomas, jun., died 1720.	700
Bromsgrove M. ...	William Peart. A.	150
Upton-upon-Severn.	Willian Hankins. A. ...	50
Netherton, near Dudley.	Richard Clark. A. ...	60
Inkborough (once a Fortnight.)	Yernold. A. ...	60
Bengeworth (once a fortnight.)	A. ...	60

Morrice Records of Nonconformists. 1716.

	Hearers.			Hearers.
1 Bengsworth. B.	60	8 Kidderminster. P. ...		—
2 Bromsgrove. P. ...	400	9 Netherton, nr. Dudley. B.		300
,, B. ...	150	10 Pershore. B.		700
3 Bewdley. P....	300	11 Sturbridge		—
,, B.	100	12 Tenbury		—
4 Dudley	—	13 Upton-on-Severn. B. ...		50
5 Eversham. P.	200	14 Worcester. P.		700
6 Inkborough (once a fortnight). B.	50	,, B. ...		400
7 Kingswood, nr. King's Norton		15 Westmacote, see Glostersh.		40

LISTS FOR 1772.

		Presb. & Indts.		Bapt.	
		Cong.	Min.	Cong.	Min.
1	Bewdley ...	2	2	1	1
2	Bromsgrove	3	3	1	1
3	Dudley ...	2	2	1	1
4	Eversham ...	2	2	1	1
5	Kidderminster	1	1		
6	King's Wood	1	1		
7	Pershore ...	1	1	1	1
8	Stourbridge	1	1		
9	Upton ...	1	1	1	1
10	Worcester	2	2	1	1

REMARKS :

"At Eversham ye Paedobaptist Congregation is of late years much reduced. The Baptists at Bengsworth, its suburbs, have a small house, but it is well filled.

At Upton there is a very neat house pretty well filled.

At Worcester the Paedobaptist is pretty large ; the Baptist rather small.

Kidderminster a very large congregation.

At Netherton, near Dudley, are a few Baptists, but no meeting house, and a Sabbatarian Congregation near Upton.

Kingswood is in King's Norton parish within seven miles of Birmingham. They never had a resident minister, but were supplied by ministers from Birmingham. They have a parsonage house and some temporalities, about £16 or £18 per annum, and have now a worthy laborious minister who lives among them and hath about 200 hearers where there used to be about 20. [Orton ; August, 1773.]

At Brettle Lane, near Dudley, there is often a meeting of Persons who call themselves Dissenters ; Lady Huntingdon's pupils often preach there. Some Baptists attend, but they are no way regular as yet, though their numbers increase."

WORCESTERSHIRE : THE MINISTERS WHO APPROVED OF AND CONCURRED IN YE LATE [*circ.* 1770,] APPLICATION TO PARLIAMENT FOR THE REPEAL OF THE CORPORATION AND TEST ACTS.

BENJ. FAWCET, Kidderminster.
JOB ORTON   ,,
DANIEL LEWIS, Kingswood.
WM. WOOD, Dudley.
J. EDGE, Stourbridge.
JOHN ASH, Pershore.
JOHN WELLS, Upton.
RICH. JENKINS, Bromsgrove.
WILLM. WELLS   ,,
JAMES BUTTERWORTH, ,,

JOHN POINTING, Worcester.
LAWR. BUTTERWORTH, Eversham.
THOS. URWICK, Worcester.
EDW. CHEWNING BLACKMORE, ,,
PAUL CARDALE, Eversham.
JOHN ADAMS, Bewdley.
JAMES VICORY   ,,
JOHN JONES   ,,
JOHN BLACKSHAW, ,,

NOTE ON THE GILLAM PAPERS.

DURING Mr. Rowley Hill's recent illness a number of papers and books relating to Angel Street Chapel, including a Minute book, cash books, and a manuscript history of the chapel, belonging to Mr. ROBERT GILLAM, an old member of the Angel Street Congregation, were by his direction sent by Mr. F. R. Jeffery of 5 Foregate Street, Worcester, to Mr. Hill. Owing to his state of health he was unable to look into them, and they were sent back by one of his daughters to Mr. Jeffery. Messrs. Southall & Co. suggested that possibly, on application from me, Mr. Jeffery would lend me the books and papers to make use of them in the work I have on hand. Upon my promising to hand them over when done with to one of the trustees of Angel Street Chapel, Mr. Jeffery has has sent me these books and papers. The minute book relates to the Evangelical Society and the Sunday School. The manuscript history corresponds with that of Mr. Blackwell of which Mr. Hill sent me a copy. But it contains a more detailed account of the unfortunate circumstances which led to the exclusion of the Rev. FRANCIS BLACKMORE from the pulpit (p. 97), in great part vindicating and exculpating him and indicating that it arose from some jealousy between the assistant, Mr. STOKES, and him. It also explains more fully the Rev. THOMAS URWICK'S resignation (p. 107) in a way perfectly honourable to him, and tells us his last sermon at Worcester was from John xx. 28, *My Lord and my God*, in which he expressly opposed the Socinian hypothesis.

As to the " financial difficulties " referred to (p. 115), and the costly Chancery suit, these Gillam papers throw considerable light. In the *MS. History* the following account is given :—

" It was discovered that the Trustees of the Meeting House were all dead but one. That a very considerable sum of money, as a residuary legacy, had been received.* That no accounts had for many years been exhibited. That no information could be obtained where the title deeds of the property were deposited. That twelve years had elapsed beyond the regular time of renewing the lease of the Meeting House, &c.

The surviving trustee being very desirous of continuing and strengthening, if possible, the constitution of the Church on its originally evangelical principles and practice, measures were taken to set matters

---

* The account book names the interest of £700 Consols belonging to the church, and £400 the Douglas legacy through the Rev. Thos. Urwick, besides other bequests.

generally to rights; but the obstinacy of an individual,* to whom all this irregularity was owing, resisting every attempt at a peaceable and candid investigation and arrangement, and refusing even to the surviving trustee the inspection of any documents relative to the concerns of the congregation, occasioned an appeal to the Court of Chancery; and an information was filed in the name of the Attorney-General.

This suit was opposed, every offer of accommodation was rejected, every means of procrastination which the practice of that court permitted were adopted, and the question never came to a judicial decision. When the general facts stated in the information had been established or admitted the quieting hand of death closed the contest."

NOTE ON THE SUNDAY SCHOOLS.

(See pp. 139-144.)

AMONG the GILLAM PAPERS (which have come into my hands since going to press) is a small quarto minute book, entitled, *Worcester Evangelical Society*, and containing information regarding the beginning of the Sunday School movement. "At a meeting of persons of different denominations, held in Angel Street Chapel, January 1, 1795, this society was formed, to encourage evangelical preaching in destitute towns and villages, to promote the instruction of the poor and ignorant, especially children, by the establishment and assistance of schools and good books." The members then were, Messrs. Osborn, Flight, Barr, Roberts, Butler, Gillam, Richards, J. Allies, R. Allies, Higgins, Russell, Edmunds, Blackwell, Whittingham, Strickland. At a meeting in Birdport Chapel, February 3, 1795, it was agreed "that the establishment

* The Chancery Bill gives the name of MARTIN BARR as defendant in the suit. He kept possession of the Books as Executor of TIMOTHY GILLAM, the church treasurer, who died in 1794.

of a SUNDAY SCHOOL in this city (to be visited by the members of this society, and to attend in rotation at the different places of worship), is a desirable object, and the Secretary, Mr. Osborn, is requested to apply for help to the London society.—April 7, 1795. That Mr. Venables be spoken to as a proper person to undertake the care of a boys', and Mrs. Ross of a girls' Sunday school, with the offer of from 1s. to 2s. per day according to the number.—May 5, 1795. On the report of Mr. Allies it was agreed to employ Mr. Venables as the master of the boys' Sunday school at the rate of 1s. for 12, 1s. 6d. for 18, and 2s. for any number above 24, and this to take place as soon as a convenient room can be procured, if not in Mr. Venables' own house.—June 2, 1795. That the Secretary endeavour to engage Mrs. Ross to teach a girls' school at the same rate as the boys'; and also to let her room for the two schools united, at least for the present. The Secretary having the prospect of visiting London soon, is requested to urge the application for the Sunday school fund.—September 8, 1795. That Mr. Barr be requested to engage a room for the Sunday school, to be opened if possible within the month. —October 14. Mr. J. Allies having offered the use of the vestry at Birdport for the Sunday School, it is thankfully accepted; and Mr. Allies is requested to engage Mr. Venables to undertake the care of the children as soon as possible. December 8.—That it is desirable speedily to engage a room for the Sunday school, as the vestry in Birdport is not thought adapted."

These resolutions seem to have come to nothing, for at a meeting of the Society in Angel Street, "February 7, 1797—Present: Messrs. Blackwell, Burden, Flight, Lewis, Osborn, Roberts; it was resolved that the idea of a Sunday school be entertained at a future meeting; and our friends are requested to attend.—April 4, 1797. That Mr. Osborn consult Mr. T. Hunt to know whether he would undertake the tuition of a Sunday school.—May 2. That as Mr. Hunt declines, the members be requested to look out a suitable person, and also for a room. That Mr.

J. Taylor be applied to as a suitable person.—June 13. That the secretary settle with Mr. CURTOIS as master of the Sunday school, on condition of his undertaking the care of any number of boys under 40, and affording room at 2s. 6d. per week ; attending himself regularly on public worship with the school at Angel Street Chapel.—August 8, 1797. At the monthly meeting of the Evangelical Society these rules for the Sunday school attending Angel Street were agreed to :—

" 1. Every boy must be recommended by some member of the Evangelical Society, and his name be inserted in a book to be kept by the master. 2. The master and scholars are to attend school at 9 o'clock every Sabbath morning. Business to begin with prayer, and then to spend until 10.30 in spelling and reading, or learning some appointed catechism or hymn. 3. At 10.30 the master and scholars (two and two) are to walk orderly to meeting, and occupy seats in the gallery without noise or inattention. 4. After the first service they are to disperse for dinner ; to meet at the school again at 1, spell and read till 2.30, thne attend public worship, after which they are to return to school till 5, and then disperse for the day. 7. The members of the society are requested to attend in rotation, two at least every Sabbath, to inspect the school. 8. All who acquit themselves diligently and well shall be rewarded either with books or some part of clothing.

" September 5, 1797—That the attendance at the Sunday school has been very pleasing for the last two Sundays. That the secretary apply to Mrs. Ross of Sidbury to undertake a girls' school, and, if she can attend the business, that she be allowed the same, *i.e.*, 2s. 6d. per week, as the master for any number not exceeding 40 girls. November 7, 1797 —That as Mrs. Ross declined the care of a girls' school, and we have neither room nor funds for the undertaking, we think it prudent at present to defer this matter.—November 22. To recommend a regular attention to the school to our friends, and that every boy reported to the visitors for ill behaviour, after three times being admonished shall be expelled. That the secretary furnish a few spelling books for present supply. That the back seat of the front gallery is very eligible for the Sunday boys, and that every visiting friend that can make it convenient be requested, not only to attend the school, but sit with the boys during public worship.—February 6, 1798. That the secretary procure catechisms for the boys. That at least one visitor be publicly requested to attend every Sabbath.—March 14. That two boys of the best progress be allowed to attend in the evening of the week days to learn writing of Mr. Curtois.—May 9, 1798. That Mr. Allies and Mr. Felton be requested to apply to Mrs. Maclean to undertake the care of a girls' Sunday school, and furnish room at the rate of 2s. per week.—June 22 Agreed to employ Mrs. MACLEAN as mistress of the girls' Sunday school, she undertaking the charge of any number not exceeding 40, and also to find room for the same at 2s. 6d. a week. That the school commence on Sunday, July 1, and be regulated by the same laws as the boys. June 12, 1799.—That the annual sermon for this Institution be preached on the last Sabbath in August next, and that suitable hymns for the occasion be prepared by the secretary.—October 2, 1899. There was collected for the benefit of this Society at Angel Street, at the annual sermon, August 25, £26 14s. 3d. ; and £2 2s. have been since received as annual subrcriptions.—November 6, 1799. That the subscriptions and collections for the Sunday School attending here be made out separately, and be kept as a distinct account in future. This was agreed to on December 4, when it was also agreed that it is highly expedient to erect and provide rooms for the convenience of the schools.—January 2, 1800. That on account of the severity of the present season, the sum of one guinea each be granted to the Master and Mistress of the Sunday schools, no regular increase of salary be allowable to either. That the amount of the several collections made at Angel Street meetings for the benefit of the schools there attending has been £47 9s. 1½d., which, with the grant from the London Society of £5 4s. for the last year, makes a total of £52 13s. 1½d., out of which there has been expended for the schools alone £36 os. 10d.—May 13, 1800. That Mrs. Maclean having declined the girls' School, Mrs. RICHARDS, of Silver Street, be elected on trial for three months at the rate of 2s. a week for tuition, and 3d. for the Room.—September 10, 1800. Present: Messrs. Evans, Gillam, Osborn, Stokes, Young, resolved that the Annual Sermons for the benefit of the schools be preached on the 3rd and 4th Sabbath of October next.—October 8. That the four most suitable girls be selected by the Visitors and Governess and be sent to learn writing from Mr. Curtois on the same footing as the boys.

That it is expedient to present the boys and girls with some useful gifts, hats, caps, tippets or stockings.—1801, February 10. That the receipt for the benefit of the Schools including the subscription and public collection, with the allowance from the London Society was £67 14s. 6d. ; the expenditure £27 14s. 2½d. ; and therefore the balance for the future support of the School is £40 os. 3½d.—February 9, 1802. That the sum of £33 11s. was collected at the Annual Meeting for the benefit of the Schools by the sermon, &c.—November 2. That no more children be admitted into either of the schools until next year, 1803. That a new pair of shoes be allowed to each boy and to each girl, to attend the Anniversary Sermon. That it seems advisable to provide new bonnets for the girls with strings, and new stockings for the boys.

The Minute Book thus runs on to September 27, 1815, on the same lines ; showing that the Sunday Schools down to that date were conducted by two paid teachers, one for the boys, the other for the girls ; that they met in hired rooms ; that visitors two by two in rotation came in to see that the rules were kept, and the teaching properly conducted ; that spelling and reading were among the subjects of instruction ; and writing on week evenings for the best scholars ; that the children received clothing every Anniversary as a reward for good attendance and behaviour, and that the effort was well supported both by annual subscriptions and the anniversary collection, when special hymns were printed and sung. Mr. Osborn (the chairman and secretary) preached the annual sermon till his death in 1812. Then Mr. Robert Gillam was chosen as secretary. Rev. J. A. James of Birmingham was requested to preach, but it does not appear that he came. The signatures to the minutes, November 19, 1812, are—

Benj. Burden.	B. Stokes.	S. Burden.
Rob. Gillam.	Sam. Pearce.	M. Barr.
Rich. Evans.	Martin Barr, junr.	Rob. Felton.
Benj. Blower.	Thos. Hodges.	Josh. Lilly.

Application at this meeting was made to the Trustees of Angel Street for the use of the vestry as a schoolroom for the girls. This was granted. In 1813 Rev. Mr. BREWER preached the annual sermon; 1814 Rev. D. FLEMING.

INDEX

OF PERSONS, PLACES, AND SUBJECTS.

(Not including all in the Parliamentary Survey, or the Non-Parochial Registers.)

.Q